Harrison Carter

How to Be A Business Owner

The Secrets to Planning and Growing a Profitable Business

CRUCIAL TREATS

USA

Contents

I

Introduction

When you think about being a business owner, it may be that so many things come to mind. The first might be the need to be a success and create a business that makes a profit. You may even be thinking about the potential roadblocks you will surely find along the way. Owning a business is challenging yet quite rewarding too. Companies everywhere aim to provide some form of value to their customers more and more leaning toward improved customer satisfaction, embracing innovation, and creating sustainable business practices. Right now, you may be in one of two camps. Perhaps you've just started your business, and you need a road map to guide you on your way. You may also be seasoned in business but would like to explore different business opportunities. In either of these cases, this book can guide you. I've spent almost a decade helping business owners come to terms with their business needs and taking their business from new to thriving in less than a year. I've observed that business owners who have a propensity for constant improvement and innovation always come out victorious.

They lead the way in getting the best employees on board, stepping forward into conflict, and growing their companies to million-dollar companies. These are the owners that eventually sell their business for large profits, and craft a significant nest egg. It's even more; I'm prone to see this come to life falling that business owners do need an extra hand and help when starting.

In this book, you can expect to find a phased approach to business where I teach you how to run your business from start to finish. In the early sections, you will learn that starting up a business is a daunting task, and you must start by managing yourself first. It would be best if you planned to succeed by setting key goals and milestones for your organization. It will become apparent that a little planning goes a long way. Once you embrace this sentiment and use the guidelines brought to you in this part of the book, you will be excited about operating your business from a strategic perspective.

Yet it's not always about strategy. A business needs great leadership. Often leadership can be confused with management. These are slightly different where leadership is about supporting, growing, and mentoring people to do the best work. It could be in line with your contractors, partners, and employees. While management ensures that the business is operating well, reporting and monitoring are in place and that you have the financial interests you have taken care of. When you have these aspects down in your business, you will immediately start to see that you have less weight on your shoulders since you have adapted yourself as a business owner to meet the needs of your company.

Another critical aspect I will be looking into is how innovation can change how your business operates and how to leverage it to bring better products and services to the market. You can expect to see those business owners who stay ahead always do so to the benefit of their company. This means they choose to put on a progressive approach to their business. This will undoubtedly serve them well in the long run.

Smart business owners also consider the reserves in their business. They look at the backups and their capacity to invest. When you can invest, you get to have more options for your business. In this section, I'll consider how successful business owners leverage investing principles to build up their reserves for a later stage. If you don't merely want to be running your business and working till you're old and grey, this part will show you how to avoid that trap and help you find a better way to approach retirement and business continuity.

Maybe you've heard the term automation, which often brings fear to many people's hearts. So in this part, you will get the opportunity to unpack automation and what it can mean for a business. You will see that it could promote less burnout in your company and also help you to focus on your strategic initiatives like growing your company to the next level. When you automate, it will help when you later feel the need to sell your company for a profit.

You can see that the parts of this book build on each other, where each takes on running a business from a different angle. In the progress and build segment, also it looks at how you can keep improving in your business, and it will show you how you can avoid the dreaded complacency that often works its way into companies. I'll show you tried and tested examples of how people are committed to continuously improving themselves and their business, operating from a learning outlook.

In the final section, my focus will be on helping you launch your business. Your business may already be in the works and running, but launching is more than merely starting. It's about commitment to apply everything you learned and watch your company grow year on year. It's imagining those milestones and then putting in the work to reach every goal. It's about the celebrations and learning and finally providing the value add to your customers in ways that you would never have imagined. This section is about action and doing the work that needs to get done, it will connect everything you learned, and you can then start by practicing.

In terms of how to navigate this book, I recommend reading it from part 1 to 9 in that order as each one builds on each other. That's not to say you won't get value from taking any section and applying what you need at the time since each part could also be standalone. You will also see action steps at the end of each piece, and these are practical tools to put what you learned into action. You may consider reading this book with a partner or like-minded person who can also walk the business path with you. My only hope is that you leverage the business secrets contained in this book, and use it to make a success of your own business. Let's get started by looking at part 1.

II
Sacrifice

Building a business is not for the faint of heart, but if you're willing to take a risk, then the rewards are great for you and your loved ones. The rewards include being able to run your own business with autonomy, and ensure that you make all of the decisions. You do not have a boss whispering in your ear and telling you what to do. You are the boss.

If your business does well, you immediately see an update in your life, which bodes well for you and your family. Imagine a world where you are running your own business and live life on your own terms. You will also have to consider and know the sacrifice it took you to get there. If you're reading this book and considering taking that leap, I have to warn you that it is not an easy path to be a business owner. You will stumble more times than you succeed, but all it takes is that one time to make it a success, that one idea. Sacrifice is a big part of getting to that big and bold success.

You may know him from his brash style and outgoing personality, but also his no-nonsense approach to business. What you don't know is that he used to be someone who played golf three times a day before he sacrificed everything to go all-in on his business. Now he is the bestselling author businessman and estimated to be worth 300 million dollars.

He says that he used to be distracted and entitled, always waiting for money to come to him, so he had to give it his all to master his craft. In that sense, he worked as many hours as it took and had up his hobbies and social status to become a titan of business. His motto merely being that he will do the things today that he may not like, but that will pave the way for a better future. His name is Grant Cardone, and he is one of the biggest business owners in the world.

Similar to Grant Cardone, many business owners take on countless amounts of stress and worry and have to keep going. It's their duty and their passion that is combined to help make a success of their business venture.

Most entrepreneurs are honestly prepared to give up their pleasure at that moment for future success they hope to see. That may seem easy when you aren't yet making the sacrifice at first, so you must understand how much is at stake and how much you must give up while moving your business to success.
The best way to move past the sacrifices is to have ample preparations, which usually means setting expectations for yourself and those around the financial needs, time needs, and action needed from your end.
In this chapter, I want to share how much you will need to sacrifice and give you a realistic idea to provide you with clarity when you eventually go into business.

You will learn:

- Financial capital
- Free time
- You are the CEO

Financial capital needed

You have to have sufficient funds before you start a business, depending on the business structure, of course. This means preparation is critical if you suddenly decide to quit your job and go solo, make sure you have six months' worth of income saved up just in case. This will give you peace of mind and also the comfort to keep going.

Yes, we have heard too many cases of people who risked it all and made a sacrifice with minimal backup capital. It was always a struggle and likely will continue to be that way for them. Even if there are financial constraints, always engage with your dependents and let them know about the potential loss of financial security. It also makes it clear that you are fully committed to the business and making it a success. Understand the exact figures of what will be needed, and this gives you an idea of what you can afford and what you cannot. Also, note down what happens with your investment should your business not be a success.

There is no way to know how much you would need exactly but always practice due diligence to ensure that you are not left stranded and having to put yourself in awkward situations where your family is at risk. You will know the signs of too little funding and aim to avoid the optimism cycle that should be steered to more realism.

You must also keep in mind that you will not make much money for the first few years of your new business. All the money you bring in will be used to build your business and improve it. Most of that money will come from you and your family. You call it an investment because you hope to see some form of reward eventually. Your sacrifice becomes much more substantial because if the money goes then, you may not have a roof over your head or means to take care of your family.

At the same time, you don't have to rely on a boss to decide how much you get paid. That said, even though entrepreneurs can get paid from their business, they choose not to pay a salary until the revenue becomes regular. Take note of this in the early stages and plan appropriately for what will happen. Know that the sacrifice will be worth it but also be realistic about how you will support your family during this time.

These are some of the typical financial sacrifices entrepreneurs have been known to make:

Credit card debt is a big one. This is the case because most banks will only lend money to businesses that have a valuable asset available. Most companies don't have that. They resort to extending the credit line and using that money to invest. Other entrepreneurs have also cashed in their 401K plans, which are somewhat like an emergency savings account. This is often used as seed capital. Finally, and this is not recommended, some business owners ended up skipping mortgage, loans, and required payments. This is often to buy time and understand the market better.

Free time

You have to know that you have to be willing to sacrifice free time to get your business running. This is a necessary aspect of owning a business that your time is no longer your own. You have to forego holidays, weekends and the usual dinner parties. This can be a huge sacrifice as a social setting, and connecting is a necessity. The good news is that if you find passion in your work, you know that sacrificing free time is worth it and more. I heard that a new business could be compared to a newborn baby.

The first is that newborn babies are prone to cry at any given moment. It will not respect that you need to sleep, have a schedule, and family commitments. Baby's demand attention and at all of the more inappropriate times too. Most importantly, you have to keep calm and keep nurturing your baby in the early stages where it's the most fragile and needs your protection. Your business is exactly like this and needs lots of time.

In many cases, I read about entrepreneurs who have tons of time; I have not yet mastered that in my business ventures. All I know is that I have people that need some form of help for my business. My free time has become nonexistent, but I like it that way because it has a purpose and fuels me to keep on going and doing my best for my business.

If you did indeed leave your 9-5 in the hope that entrepreneur life would be more comfortable than I'm afraid it's the wrong perception. If you want freedom, you have it, but it's also necessary to take all of the risks. Sleep deprivation has become a prominent thing in business owners, and especially in the early stages. Later on when they are thriving like Elon Musk and Jeff Bezos, then they look less sleep-deprived, but I would imagine that they have better coping mechanisms now.

You are the CEO

You are the CEO; the existence of the business will rely on you. You are the anchor. Yes, you may need a team, but you are the captain. Success will be driven by the actions you make. This usually happens because even if you are not actively working at your business or doing business tasks, you will likely always be thinking about it. People start to wonder if you are mentally present in the conversations. That's due to the responsibility you have to take on and keep the business moving. You have to think about stocks, employees, orders, and more. There's not a lot of room for other modes of thought. Not to mention the consistent problem solving and brainpower needed at every turn. You may feel victorious on one day, only to be down in the gutter on the next day.

You'll feel like you're on a rollercoaster that is going 1000 miles per hour and then it slows only before it takes you down a new winding path. You have to be prepared for these aspects of the business. That said, it can be the best thing you will ever do. Every day will bring you newfound purpose and joy in your life. You'll have to prepare in advance and avoid games that don't grow your mindset, remove television, and other activities that are not directly helping your business to succeed. Breaks are also necessary, so use them well, and the best way is to spend time with loved ones and make their day as unique as possible. Know it's the little moments where you give the most attention that counts.

That's ultimately where your time management skills can play a significant role, becoming a valuable tool that helps to ensure you have everything under control and giving you the headspace you need while growing your business.

Risk

Please keep in mind that a new business requires tons of risk, which usually means you have to sacrifice security and your stability. As I mentioned earlier, you will have more financial worries than the ordinary person, but there will be more benefits in the long run. If you came into the business with an excellent reputation, you might find that you have a fear this will get lost along the way.

This reputation gets lost as businesses are prone to fail in the early stages, and that's why they can eventually be successful. Without failures, a company doesn't learn everything and will set the business up for risk later down the line. I would imagine that this pressure can feel unsettling, and it's so hard to focus when you feel overwhelmed and that there is no way out of the obstacles. Many business owners do take lots of risks, and this can usually look like it's for no good reason.

That's why it becomes so important to always prepare in advance, especially if you have dependents. Consider how it will be if you risk everything, but you are responsible for other people's lives. It may seem glamorous to take a risk at that moment, but when everything goes wrong, you may just regret it. To avoid that regret, it's a good idea to outline everything needed in your business, so you know exactly what's at stake and can prepare your family for it. It's critical to have frank discussions with your loved ones to plan for potential failure. If you have a business partner, think of it as a strategic meeting and finding out the fall-out plan and the risk factors at present.

It goes without saying that the better you understand the ways your business could fail, the more prepared you are for the success and the failures, and you will always be able to get back up again. It's a mindset of accepting the risk, understanding that its part of your business dreams, and navigating your stress and worry. It's easier said than done, but with time and effort, you will see results.

What should not be sacrificed?

While sacrifices must be made, entrepreneurs or business owners must choose not to make the following sacrifices:

Your health - As much as sleep will be sacrificed, aim not to have a lack of sleep for extended periods. Sacrificing your health for the sake of your business can be counterproductive. If a business owner is sacrificing their health and surviving on minimal sleep and a bad diet, the company may not last that long. The overworked and exhausted entrepreneur is a tale as old as any, but many business owners are showing it does not need to be that way. They are showing that getting sufficient sleep, exercise, and having a proper diet makes you effective at running your business. Entrepreneurs such as Jack Dorsey and Richard Branson have decided that their health comes first. Jack Dorsey of Twitter may be slightly extreme in his approaches such as rigorous fasting and meditation habits. Yet he maintains that he has to run two companies and needs to be in the best shape at all times. He journals and loves to track his sleep patterns. You could say that while some of his habits are strange, they help him to be the most productive he can be.

On the other hand, there is Richard Branson, who also ensures he keeps as healthy as possible. He always prioritizes enough sleep, and that's between 5-6 hours. More than that, he has a morning and night routine, which he is religious about following. He finds that having a structure in his day helps to start and finish the essential tasks that need to get done in a day. For him, balance is critical, but not the same way as other people. He knows he only has 24 hours a day, so he must make the most of his every waking hour. That said, he also know-hows essential it can be to experience joy and laughter in his evenings. He makes it his priority to always enjoy dinner with family and friends in the evening, and he finds that where he gets his best ideas from. He also takes some time away from his phone, and unplugging is vital to mental health.

What are some of the take outs here?

It's likely a good idea that instead of doing the last bit of paperwork by pulling an all-nighter, you should just go to bed. Do yourself a huge favor and wake up early and take it on in the morning. The morning time is when you are likely to be the most alert and alive to possibility, and you will get more done. Compare it to night time where your brain is too tired to do anything more. You will make more mistakes, and that will cost you in the long run.

If you are going to be busy, take comfort in the fact that exercise, good sleep, and a healthy diet will bring you many benefits when added to your schedule. This will invigorate you and help to improve your overall outlook on your projects ahead. Simple ways to do this is to multitask by meal planning on Sundays and also take quick workouts during lunch breaks.

Key takeaways

- Starting a business involves significant amounts of sacrifice; you have to give it your all and may not see any rewards for extensive periods. You should go all in, and understand the risks before leaping.
- Money is a driving factor in starting a business. Think about all of the money you will need to fund your business, pay salaries, and keep the business running. Companies can take time to make a profit eventually.
- Your weekends will have to stand by the wayside in your business as there is no free time. Even your family may

need to keep in mind that your work will be your life until you can succeed.

- You will need to be everything for your business. In other words, being called the CEO means you are the anchor who will need to take charge, make the right decisions, and take action. Without you, there is no business.

Actions steps

1. Make a list of all your responsibilities and also the time allocated to these activities. You may need to then discuss each of these with your significant other to find out better ways to manage those activities. Auditing your time in the early stages of running a business, will help when you get started and free up your time.
2. Become better at prioritizing by investing in tools that help you operate on schedule, and cut out all time wasters like streaming, gaming and activities that will not directly affect growing your business.
3. Set up time daily or weekly to get a sense of how your fault is coping with the new business arrangements then discuss how to improve.

Being a business owner will bring sacrifice into your life, but you can choose how you make that sacrifice. It helps to remember that your family or loved ones play a vital role in your overall motivation and they must get the related communication from your end, to understand the expectations of how the business life will go. It's especially important when you have left a well-paying job and were used to certain comfort levels.

You have to learn to live with less temporarily in favor of what your business could be. Remember that real success is never without sacrifice. Think about how Grant Cardone decided to change his life and sacrifice his social life and hobbies for a better experience and how that turned out for him. He can safely call himself someone who lives in a new life filled with everything his heart desires, and it takes time, diligence, and sacrifice.

Sacrifice is essential, but balance is valuable, so always ensure that you take a leaf out of Richard Branson's book and make time for the people you love, and give them your undivided attention. This is how you stay invigorated in your business. While sacrifice and balance are essential, it's also a good idea to look at what will drive you when things are not going your way. Some call this passion, and that's exactly what I want to discuss in the next chapter of this book.

III
Passion

Passion seems to be a mythical concept but that is not always the case. It's more valuable than you know. Imagine being an entrepreneur for 30 years who has created a successful business. How would you have become successful? Did you think it was a passion that was the number one factor?

Perhaps starting, most business owners have a need and a passion for succeeding in business. This same passion was the reason behind wanting to achieve and avoid failure. Business owners learn things that may have been hard at the time, but they had to do it. Some entrepreneurs hate public speaking or website design, but they knew that it was a valuable skill to learn in business. Nowadays, you could get away with not having either of those skills, but back then, it was necessary.

The point I want to make is that even if you dislike certain aspects and tasks, you have to do those tasks because of your passion that lies in being successful. That drives you and will help you overcome all the things you hate and help you to embrace those tasks because you know why you are doing what you are doing.

So it goes without saying that you should find your passion and go all in. At the same time, you should consider your differentiator from other businesses in your industry. What makes you stand out from others offering the same products and services?

To understand your differentiation factor, we must look to other passion-based businesses and look at how they started with the concept of "Why."

Almost two decades ago, a little known business owner who specialized in marketing spoke using flip chart paper and a passion for his ideas. In his talk, he promptly said: "Here's how Apple communicates," and that was enough to get us into an understanding of why Apple has such a strong following, and that's because Apple starts with the "Why" of their business. The "Why" comes before the "How" and the "What" of their business.

They know that the "why" is the most valuable part of what they are offering, and people don't care about what you do. They care about why you do it, as Simon Sinek promptly told us in his now-famous Ted Talk.

Let's talk about Apple and why they do what they do. In the '70s, when Apple first came up, Steve Jobs, the founder, aimed to make a personal computer, one that was not the size of a room. He had exuberance and passion knowing a personal computer should not be anything special, but merely another appliance in the home. This passion drove everything they did, from creating the iPod to designing our smartphone interface that we now take everywhere.

Passion based businesses like Apple have a burning purpose that lights the CEO's up, and that makes their message palatable. Again it rings true to what Simon Sinek said: people, don't buy what you do. They buy why you do it.

You will learn:

- Be passionate or don't create a business at all
- Love what you do, and you will never work a day in your life
- Owning a company should be a motivating force for you

Be passionate

You should only do it if you are passionate about the business. Know that a company takes effort, time, and sacrifice to get it started. Most companies will fail, and the business owners will head back to their jobs to try again. The companies that do make it will have gone through tons of failure. Successful business owners have to be resilient. How does one keep going when all else is falling apart around them? It's a matter of the deep-rooted passion and enthusiasm business owners have from within.

They store it deep down because they want to make a difference in the world. It becomes a need and a fire that grows within them to take their idea to the world. When you are passionate about what you do, people notice this. When you are relaxed about what you do, people also see.

People want to follow those who are passionate about the product or service the business is selling. They want you to energize them and show them how what you created can help them. The world is filled with problems, and it's a problem solver who looks at those problems optimistically, getting their attention, and getting people to buy their products.

People may not always be passionate about what they are selling, but they are excited that their product brings value to their customers. They know that when their products sit in their customer's hands, it will bring relief, joy, and happiness for a problem that has been ailing them for so long. This is where the idea of passion comes from; it comes from serving people and giving them your best to help them.

Many people I speak to want to know if they can learn passion, or is it something that business people innately possess. That's not true; your passion is always inside of you; it just needs to be ignited and drawn out. It needs to make you get up and take action. Let's think about the company Amazon. You know and love that they always deliver straight to your door and can even do it in a day. Did you know that Jeff Bezos was extremely passionate about his idea, and he saw it on a grand scale from day 1?

He always wanted Amazon to be an "Everything Store." Amazon now has everything you can imagine. It even bought Whole Foods so you can get healthy foods amidst everything else. Could he have done it without being passionate about what he did? That's certainly a no. You see, when it started, Amazon did not see much profits for close to 10 years, and even then, they were barely getting by. Their shares were mediocre and quite inexpensive, and Jeff Bezos and his executive team would have to pack books in the early stages of Amazon as it was too expensive to hire people.

Additionally, Bezos left a well-paying job in corporate America to head up Amazon at the time. They lost money and lots of it, but they needed to keep going. This vision was driven by Jeff's passion and enthusiasm to keep going, knowing that he could serve people.

Now, Amazon has the highest share price, and it has the most prominent online retail store in the world. Being passionate makes a difference; it takes you through the tough times and helps you keep going even when your business has not seen profits. It makes you work within your company because you know that it can and will be something. It's an invisible thread that only you can see.

We can safely say that being passionate about your business can be the catalyst for your business to succeed. When a mediocre idea has a passionate business leader, it can become game-changing. Even so, when a great idea meets a passionate business owner, it can reach new heights. Therefore aim to seek out spaces where you can be intense and make it your duty to always work in an area you are passionate about.

Love what you do

If it's something you love, then it's a no brainer. If you're going to hate your life after starting, stay away from said business. Doing something just for the money does not bode well for you and the people you will eventually hire.

I can tell you what will happen to you:

- You will hate going into work every day, which will frustrate you and lead to poor relationships.
- It will make your home life even worse because you are not fulfilled by the work you do, and that will create a considerable distance in your family.
- You will procrastinate most of the work until everything piles up, and your business's workload massively stresses you.

Overall, you should love what you do so you can avoid being disappointed in life. Loving what you do doesn't mean loving every aspect of your business; it is about appreciating everything knowing that it will move the needle. It means your business has you working at it knowing you will get to the point of success. Everything is a matter of hard work, tenacity, urgency, and drive to do the impossible.

Here's what will happen when you love what you do:

- Waking up to go to work will be a joy, and you will spring out of bed, ready to take on the day.
- You will be the most enthusiastic person in the building, and people who work with you will admire your optimism and will feel the energy to do more for the business.
- Since you are so satisfied at work, your home life is pleasurable, and you always enjoy every minute
- Work doesn't feel like work, it feels fun and exciting, and every minute brings a new experience to you and the people who work with you.
- It shows up on the bottom line, your customers will love you, and what your business stands for, so they will keep coming back for the service you give with a smile.

Often when a company loves what they do, it comes from the top down. That usually means the owner and the employee's feel it. Recent studies show that companies where the owner loves their business and what they offer will say they love their jobs. They will tell anyone who will listen. They will also post it on social media and make friends who do not work at the company, jealous of such a great workplace.

Business owners were prompted and were asked why they love their business. They shared the following reasons:

- Each day has variety, and no two days are ever the same in any way. It's exciting, and it gets them going.
- They get to help people do something amazing and put a smile on their face
- It's such a great feeling to know you created something from scratch that didn't exist before they did.

- Their business allows them to be the master of their destiny.

These are just a few reasons people love their business, and of course, the list can be longer than this. You should also consider why you love your business. Think about how it makes you feel? Do you feel enthusiastic when you wake up in the morning, and are you excited to tackle another day? These telltale signs that you have a passion for what you do, and it will drive you to success.

If not, it always helps to consider if it's a trend or a once-off feeling. You may simply be in a slight slump; every business owner has their ups and downs, and you could be the same. If there are more downturns than upturns, then it's time to consider if the path is right for you. Reflect, contemplate, and take action to make a change.

Owning a business should be a motivating force

Owning a business should motivate you. It should get you out of bed in the morning. There shouldn't be the feeling of snoozing your alarm. You should feel as though your business is exciting, and you cannot wait to do some amazing things you had planned.

Well, you cannot always be excited about every task in your business. For starters, some people hate doing taxes, but it's also necessary to do the taxes. Others don't enjoy writing; some are not fans of too much detail. But these are necessary for a business and also an essential aspect of keeping the momentum going of running a business. Without these tasks, you could not have distinctive elements like seeing your business finally make a profit and succeeding. That's why you need a driving force that is intrinsic to you and keeps you going when times get tough.

One of the ways to describe it would be having intrinsic motivation in what you do. This gives you the energy to do the mundane tasks because you love the feeling of achievement and getting work done. You know that this work will improve your business and result in expansion and growth.

Intrinsic motivation will keep you going when everyone around you has long since quit and moved to a new project. You stay the course knowing that hard work and determination will yield the best results.

It's fascinating to consider what pushes people to start a business and make a success of their lives. They know the risk and sacrifices involved but do it anyway. That means they have to have a driving force from deep within them, that grabs their attention and pushes them to start that business. Remember that starting a business takes so much money(even your retirement savings), requires many hours of hard work, patience, and knowing you may lose all of that money along the way. It's a reality that approximately 30 percent of small businesses will shut their doors within the first two years.

Let's take a moment to understand what makes people start a business in the first place:

They often want more business involvement. Perhaps they were managers in the company who employed them and decided they wanted to make the critical decisions, and that leads them to branch out.

Another reason relates to the fact big corporations can tend to be so impersonal over time. Maybe an entrepreneur started in the company when it was small, and they loved that sense of culture and close-knit community, and they don't enjoy that anymore.

Therefore they decide to create a space of community by starting their own small business.

A more significant driving force is business owners want to be responsible for decision making; they want autonomy in their business. They want their bold vision to be the one that takes them to the direction they need to go. In other words, they want the sight of most processes like marketing, product development, research and development, and customer engagement. Being a business owner, in this sense, can help them get involved.

Business owners can also start their firms because they need additional funds. Their current job does not offer them the remuneration they seek. Therefore they will start something on the side and make that a reality for themselves. If it does well enough, they leave the company and go full time in their own business.

There are many driving forces to start a business, and the reality is that you must have some motivating factor to keep you going, especially during the tough times of business. If it doesn't feel motivating or you don't have the intrinsic drive, you may fall victim to low engagement in the activity. This is one of the telltale signs to look out for.

Key Takeaways

- "Be passionate or don't create a business at all" is an attitude towards your business that will encapsulate how you go about running your company. It will show in everything you do, and it's true when people say that they can sense enthusiasm and engagement in everything you do. It's how your business can stand out from the crowd and how you get people to continue to follow you, buy from you and buy into what you do.

- Love what you do, and you will never work a day in your life is often a common phrase people use. It's quite right when you love your work, and the type of value you give to people becomes addictive, and you want to keep on doing it. You do your best to ensure your business succeeds so that people can get that same value over and over again. When you love what you do, others will also love what you do, and your business will grow extensively.
- Owning a company should be a motivating force for you, and it should drive you every day. You should be that person that as soon as you wake up, the world knows you mean business. You are so busy but also productive because you have a sense of intrinsic motivation that spurs you on every day. If you have employees, then those people are inspired by what you do and give that same impression to your customers.

Actions steps

- To ensure that you are following your passion instead of a trend, engage with those closest to you like a mentor or family member and find out what they think you are passionate about. If it matches up with your own ideas then it may be something to pursue.
- Think about your previous work experience, and how invested you were in your work. If you were heavily invested, think about what made you so. If you were not heavily invested, also consider why that was so. This will link to which processes help you stay engaged.
- Cultivate a sense of intrinsic motivation, by taking a moment each day to see how your rewards play a role in your happiness of a task. Where external rewards were a driving force, then look at how this may be harming your

progress. Opt for a more internal sense of reward like progress and let that fuel you.

Every business must start with why. Every business owner must connect with that "why" and know exactly why their business does what it does. Consider how Apple's "why" is so strong that people don't always buy what they sell, but why they sell it. You have to consider your business "why," and you do it by checking in on your passion levels for your business.

Do you wake up every day knowing that your business is going to be the next Apple or Amazon? It matters because it can impact how you create new products and services. If you're passionate about your business, people can sense it a mile off just think about how Steve Jobs amassed cult-like status with his Apple launches. Just as important as passion is that you love what you do. Sure, you may not always like every task, but you should wake up with a spring in your step ready to take on the day's challenges.

Motivation is always an inside job; you must ensure that you are driven by your business success and the work you are doing to succeed. Keep in mind that every bit helps, every moment and every action. That means you can always find the motivation in the smallest of tasks.

These critical aspects of passion, love, and motivation are the driving stones that will ensure you keep going when times are not in your favor. People always look to the leader for direction, and you have to create a team that will drive your vision and keep things moving. You cannot do it alone. The good news is that you have cultivated your sacrifice and passion muscles, and now it's time to get into the finer details of team effort and how that can positively explode your business profits.

IV

Team Effort

Going solo does not help any business, and being the lone ranger will not serve you or the company you hope to run. You must always seek out the help you need and swiftly aim to build up the team you need. This will involve a level of recruitment, and also techniques to find the right people. Also, you need to know which roles will add value to your business.

The team needs high levels of teamwork to get many tasks done, and the better the collaboration is the better, the organization will perform. That's why you have to cultivate this in your organization. To have a meaningful and lifelong business, the bottom line is that you have to work well with others in a professional and even personal context.

When there is a team effort, you will ideally see those new ideas come up all the time instead of feeling that you have to draw out insights. People on your team will bring them to you. As you know, every business needs new and fresh ideas to continue to succeed in the competitive world of business. I'm sure your business is not any different. Innovative thinking is even better when enterprises seek out and recruit a diverse team of people who can contribute their fantastic ideas.

Perhaps your business has been in a position where it had to solve massive problems, but for some reason, you were not getting anywhere. There was stagnation. Team efforts actually can help you solve problems and curb stagnation. This aspect of collaboration is vital within a group and can bring new solutions to old problems. Often companies choose to use brainstorming activities to get people creating, so working as a team can push the best ideas to the surface.

Most business owners love to work in a team environment as it can be very motivating and supportive. When you have a team effort, the team starts to hold each other accountable and ensure deadlines get met, and everyone delivers a high standard of work.

When the team genuinely cares for each other when one is behind on their work, the others rally together and pick up the slack and help.

We all know that together everyone achieves more, which will ultimately make the business run more efficiently. Teams that work together develop a bond, and that only strengthens their effort at the office. This can sometimes be known as a sense of camaraderie or morale.

Teamwork and effort are a grounding force in many people's day as they want to feel like they are contributing something to a bigger purpose and those they are valued.

Keep in mind when you leverage the strengths of your team, everyone gets to do what they love and feel encouraged by this fact too. This improves employee engagement and overall productivity. When people are confident, they will always want to do more, and knowing they make a big part of the team is even better. The sense of belonging is unmistakable.

You will learn:

- Confirm what you need to do
- Hire a team of professionals
- Principles to handle people
- How to make people like you

Confirm what you need to do

Figure out what needs to be done. Usually, this would entail a vision that has been created by you and your team. You would set this out into strategic steps, and set out the plan that would help meet the goals for your business. This would usually be the planning stage and needs your time and effort to gather all the data you have on each task and the roles required. Initially, you would have been the only person doing most of the work. Now, it's about creating roles in your organization that can take over some of the responsibilities.

Hire a team of professionals

You can quickly get people to work in your organization, but if you are not willing to invest time, money and training to get the right people, you will have a team of people that are not suited to what you are trying to build up. That's a fact. You must hire a group of people who you know will get the job done efficiently, which will give you peace of mind.

Here's how you can hire the best people for your team:

1. The business works best when you do not hire friends or family. It can be tough when you start trying to cut costs. It will pay off long term when you look out for professionals

that are not related to you. It indeed brings more complexity to your work environment than there needs to be.

2. Always have a good job description that gives candidates and internal people in your company an idea about what the job will entail. In doing so, you will ensure that the person you hire knows exactly what to do, and it does not overburden others in your organization. This certainly helps in having a robust hiring process where you ensure that the person you bring in is a good job fit. You don't want to be hiring for the same role consistently, it can be quite disruptive for your business.

3. Skills are essential, but it's also noted that skills can be taught, provided you have the best standard operating procedures in place. It's best to even look at attitude and the mindset of the individual. It may be hard to pick up at the interview stage, so always ask questions directed at the mindset and pull out scenarios that will test how they will react.

4. Get good at interviewing people. This skill often gets missed when the focus is on looking at resumes and trying to find the best candidate. Therefore, find ways to learn about how to interview better by taking a course via LinkedIn or Udemy, which is either low cost or free if you start with a LinkedIn trial.

5. Consult your current executive team if you have one, and also bring them into the interview to test if it was the right choice. They may have a different view on the matter entirely.

6. Seek out references from their previous employers, and get a sense of how well your candidates will work in a team. Often you will get to hear more details about the candidate and can make a more informed decision.

Once you hire the best people, you should aim to always treat them with care, dignity, and respect so that they can enjoy their work. Gallup is an employee engagement company that shows employees are not engaged at work, which affects productivity and profits. Since you will be working with Millennials and Gen Z in the future, it helps to know how to manage them for the best output.

Here are a few tips to guide you along the way:

- Aim to have a positive attitude towards your team. It's good to keep in mind that your team will be either energized or demoralized by your mood. Even though you may not always have good days, aim to mitigate any challenges by keeping stress free. Help and try to see things from your team's perspective so that they can build up a good relationship with you as their leader.
- Understand that your employees will be curious about "why" something is the way it is, so aim to educate and clarify their questions. They will respect you more for it.
- Don't always make it about work, treat the team, and celebrate the milestones extensively when something great happens.

In his now profound and wildly popular book How to Win Friends and influence people, Dale Carnegie talks extensively about how you can always help you team and handle them appropriately for the best results.

Principles to handle people

People always want to know you care about them but in an authentic manner. If they can sense that you don't care, they will only work half-heartedly and give the bare minimum. Initially, when the concept of a corporation became a thing in the US, initiated by the Ford Motor Company, people were hired to do very automated tasks, and they did it while working in an assembly line. During that time, they had to clock in and clock it.

There was not much autonomy, and there wasn't a need for relationship building. Therefore the managers of the time simply called out orders, and it was completed. Things have since changed immensely.

Yes, we still have hierarchies, and there are managers and leaders, but people do not want autocratic leaders (where they are too structured, and it's a commanding environment). People prefer more transformative leaders who seek to support, teach, and help people get better.

So as a business owner, you must expose yourself to the best ways to be a transformational leader who is thoroughly handling people well.

1. We've all had a boss who criticizes their team in front of everyone. It makes people become fearful of the workplace and creates a terrible environment for everyone. Add in that you get a poor reputation too. Therefore it's best not to complain and always give negative feedback to employees. The truth is that we're all human, and we will make mistakes. You are not any different. Something profound happens in an employee's brain when you criticize them, they start to become demoralized, and the opposite of what you want to happen happens. They will end up resenting you and complaining at every chance they get. If you're going to get results and a happy team, then instead smile and find ways to tell people how well they are doing. They will appreciate it and work harder along the way.

2. Aim to be sincere when providing feedback on work performance. Appreciation can light up a person's day, but when someone knows it is not genuine, it will not help them at all. Being honest and sincere in your appreciation can be a powerful catalyst to improve your employee's performance. When recognition is real, you must show that you took the time to observe the employee, and it is coming from a place of honesty and kindness.

3. The truth is often the case that people want to have enthusiasm for the work they do; they want to wake and up and feel excited about what they will achieve for that day. That's only normal, we all crave that. Yet, did you know it all starts with the business owner and how you bring up eagerness within that person? If you want to get people to do their best work, you absolutely must stop thinking about yourself and see things from their perspective. It then becomes a matter of having a win-win situation, where their wants and our wants can join forces and increase business revenue.

As you can tell, handling people well is fundamental to ensuring you meet business objectives, but this is a concept that has plagued leaders for centuries. Let's take a look at the next section and find out how to make people like you as a business owner.

How to make people like you

People can either like you or hate you, but you have the power as a business owner to make it so. If you want people to like you, there are a few guidelines that can help you out.
It's a somewhat practical guide that business owners can follow.

1. It's common knowledge that you will win more favor when you take an interest in people and the things they like.

People don't often care about much until you show them that you are sincerely interested in what they do, their hobbies, their families, and even their pets. You can do this in the first place by asking questions and getting to know people. Many in your organization worked there for years, and nobody took an interest in them, so imagine if you do. That will make a lasting difference and create positive working relationships. Start small and ask people about their day and then work your way towards more critical questions. Bonus is if you can remember people's names the next time you meet them.

2. Aim to be intentionally happy all the time. How do you show happiness? You keep a smile on your face no matter the stuff happening around. Life will always have challenges, but if you choose to be happy, you can create a positive space in your mindset. Smiling is a free way to make people feel great about their work and the company. It comforts people when the owner is smiling.

3. People's names are the way we recognize who they are, but a person's name is very important to them. If you don't remember their name, it can make them feel less important, which can make your employees disengaged and think you do not care. Studies even show that people care about their name so much they will pay good money to have their name plastered on a building. It's their legacy, and it's essential to be recognized. How do you do that if you have many employees? Always keep an organogram of your team, and whenever you speak to someone new, then aim to use their name a few times in your conversation, and by the 4th or 5th time, it would be committed to memory.

4. Be known as the entrepreneur who listens to his team instead of liking the sound of their voice. Pay attention to people when they are speaking and nod gently to affirm when they are talking. Aim to keep eye contact and

reassure the person you are speaking to. Speaking to the point we mentioned early, aim to smile when it's appropriate as it also can go a long way. Always check for understanding by summarizing what was said, as this will make the person you are speaking to feel heard. A good listener is also an encourager who draws people out of their shell and gets them to speak and feel heard.

5. The above ideas are all core to helping people feel like they matter in your business. They are not merely a number in the organization but someone essential to the running of your company. Always try and put yourself in your employee's shoes and aim to treat your team well and how you would love to be treated. Simple gestures mean a lot to people and can help them to feel important such as allowing them to speak their mind or sincerely encouraging them about the excellent work they did.

Key takeaways

- Confirm what you need to do is vital in planning your way forward for your business. Since you need a good team around you, you must ensure you have the best role definition done and also allocate tasks appropriately. Proper research will help you define everything that needs to be completed, and what other companies in your industry need to run a business. It may take some time and effort on your part but will pay off in the long term.
- Hiring a team of professionals is the best way to move forward. You want to make sure you have the best people on the side with you; they can help you meet your business's needs. We always recommend that you take time with your search, and do thorough checks and interviews to make sure you bring in the best candidates for the role. This

due diligence will pay off in the long run. You can easily find good people using LinkedIn and by leveraging your current networks.

- Principles to handle people are foundational to ensure you always support your team to do their best work. If you've ever worked for a terrible boss, you will know how demoralizing it can be to go to work every day. By applying these principles, your subordinates will appreciate your efforts and go the extra mile for you and your business.
- How to make people like you is a question that is often asked—it's all about speaking to people how they would like you to talk to them. You must always engage people, and become an authentic human being, and show a vital interest in them. In this way, they can see that you care for them and want to help them to achieve their goals.

Action steps

- Create roles in your business by researching other businesses in your industry. Look at their jobs section where they will usually include a description of each role.
- Hire individuals that will compliment your skillset, and find them in a variety of spaces like LinkedIn or hiring sites or through connections.
- Educate yourself on leadership daily, so you can provide your team with the support they need. Cultivate the traits shared in this part about how you can improve your leadership skills.

Team effort is the glue that keeps a team together and helps people do their best work. But even the best teamwork fails when the leader doesn't lead and manage them effectively. It's critical to understand that people make a difference, and they do matter. As a business owner, you have to wear many different caps, and leadership is one of them.

If you ignore the leadership aspect of your role, you will be missing out on gaining the respect, enthusiasm, and productivity of your team. Know that no business owner can achieve great success alone. Think about every successful business and how they brought in professionals to help run the business effectively. Investing in your business and team will make a big difference in the long term longevity of your organization. It does mean you have to take a step back and see where you are falling short in employee leadership. I know one thing for sure: when you begin to do it, you will notice the difference in your mindset, your team's efficiency, and your business.

Knowing that you can grow when you have a good team is a notable aspect of running a successful business, but improving your knowledge can be helpful. In the next part, we will explore how you can maximize your learning and use it to build your business and make massive profits along the way.

V
Knowledge Is Power

It's helpful to look at knowledge as future equity that will yield multiple opportunities for you in the long run. You will see this in the income you generate from the knowledge you invested in for both you and your team.

Therefore you should educate yourself and your team so you can grow your business. Just like an investment, it will bring you all sorts of unexpected opportunities along the way. Consider what you can ultimately achieve by investing in online courses, business team certification, and university opportunities. Yes, it may cost you money now, but you will always get that back in your business in many multiples.

You will learn:

- Reading this book
- Knowledge is wealth
- There is nothing more valuable than knowledge

Reading this book

Know that reading this book is the first step in being knowledgeable enough to start a business. Investing in your education will be the smartest thing you ever do. When you decided to read his book you opened pathways in your mind that will help you find new ways to be successful in your business. Perhaps your business isn't doing as well as you want it to. It's been struggling, and it's evident that whatever you have been trying has failed. You feel despondent and demotivated too.

I can assure you that by opening this book, you have taken that feeling of despondency and also used the reading tool to eradicate it. It's impossible to feel the sense of gloom when you have the blueprint for running your business in your hand, one that tells you are the tools, resources, and secrets that you may not have heard about before. The good news is you made the decision to open this book. Simply if you continue reading and get to the end you will have pumped yourself with knowledge from various areas of business using practical examples and also tools to help you see a hopeful future for what you will eventually do with your business.

Just like you opened this book, and when you are done reading you will apply these tools and see results. You can also get another book and start to build a habit of knowledge within you. It used to be that reading was the only way to get information. If you think of the business books in history that shared important business principles like the 7 habits of highly effective people, Purple Cow, and Good to Great. Each book brings with it new insights and undiscovered treasures that will serve to inspire you and bring new ideas to your business. They are packed with advice on mindset, tools, and ways to start thinking creatively in business. You know business is always changing at the speed we cannot even imagine. Things look pretty different from how they looked before but the one important thing to know is that the foundations of entrepreneurship never change too dramatically. It pays to read the great books that have paved the way for many business owners like Elon Musk, Grant Cardone, and Steve Jobs.

Knowledge is wealth

You may be wondering what it means to say that Knowledge is wealth. Surely picking up a book and reading it will not automatically qualify you for wealth. Indeed, it needs a sense of action from your end. In others, you have to do something with that knowledge. That usually means you need to apply the knowledge.

Typically you can apply your knowledge in many areas of your business, perhaps you're a small business owner then learning web design becomes a valuable skill because you can then improve your website and improve the overall traffic to your website. If you understand online Search Engine Optimization principles you can also start to engineer your website for search so that people who would need your product or service find you.

While we may know many people who have tons of knowledge and know everything about everything, most of them actually can make that conversion of knowledge and turn it into wealth. The knowledge that you have is innate and must be turned into energy or a skill that allows you to make something or provide a service. Your actual knowledge is a subset of memory, learning ability and research, and reading. It could relate to the stuff you've done in your previous job or current business.

Yet, I find that you have to find ways to add value with your knowledge, else it lays dormant in your head hoping to be used one day. If you think about Sherlock Holmes, he had pages and pages of books and he is filled with knowledge. That said, his knowledge would not be much use if there wasn't a need for his services. That is the reason he can be so good at solving crimes in his fictional world. He makes connections because he knows more and in doing so he solves more problems than others and benefits.

You must, therefore, look at your knowledge as an asset, and must go about optimizing your knowledge so that it will bring you monetary gains soon.

The big question all business owners are faced with is how do they get people to give them some financial compensation for their knowledge.

Let's unpack a few examples as a starting point:

- The market place always decides if the knowledge you are bringing to the marketplace is valuable or not. You sometimes need to take the initiative to package your knowledge into something that will bring value to people. Think about the iPhone. It is a device but if nobody knew how to use it or what it could do, it would be worthless. Since people have come to understand that smartphones make their lives easier and the iPhone is one the most secure phones, they understand the value proposition and will part with the money. The knowledge of various industries had to be sourced and joined together to bring the iPhone to life, and it all started with a vision from Steve Jobs to bring smart devices to people. His knowledge and team created a product, educated people on how it works, and brought it to the market and so the market decided to buy it. This is one example of how knowledge can be translated.
- Another example to consider is Uber, and how they disrupted the transit industry. At first, they knew that people were challenged by the state of public transport.

They also knew how to create an application. The founders also found out that you could become an intermediary of service just like how Amazon is with retail goods. In doing so, they then transformed their knowledge of app development, people's unhappiness, and modeling Amazon's business idea to form Uber. You can also notice how it was crucial that Uber merged a variety of knowledge forms to create their wealth. At present Uber is worth $90 billion.

- Knowledge is also about bringing people together to support and enhance your business. As an entrepreneur, you cannot do everything else you will burn out. Having the foresight to know that bringing in technical people and skilled professionals make a difference. This knowledge of managing people then becomes important so that you can support the talented people you bring in to help you run your company for profits. In this example, you then leverage knowledge for future wealth. At the same time, your employees are leveraging their knowledge for job satisfaction and financial gain.

Knowledge can bring wealth when applied and also knowledge can bring vibrancy and enthusiasm to you as a business owner. When you have the energy you will then seek out to do more with your knowledge. Eventually, you will find a way to create value with your knowledge down the line.

There is nothing more valuable than knowledge

I want to illustrate to you in this section how nothing is more valuable than knowledge in the world and I'll be sharing a few choice examples to do this as well. As a starting point, let's consider aspects of your life that you can possess. You can be in ownership of a car, house, money, health, and love. But there is one thing that can happen to each of these. The first is that they can be taken away from you, Your house and car can be stolen, or repossessed if you cannot afford it and if life gets somewhat tough. You could also become unwell, and there may not be a cure for your illness so your good health may go. While we would love relationships to last forever, also love can be taken away. If you look at the knowledge you possess, once you acquire it, you always have it.

Think about your degree that you acquired, it will always be the knowledge that you possess and be inherent to you. Similarly, all the skills and knowledge you're learned will stay with you no matter what happens in your business.

Consider how rapidly technology has moved and how many ordinary items it has replaced and continues to replace. The smartphone was able to replace the standard phones at home, voice recording devices, cameras, torches, and many other items. The replacement of the devices means instead of paying large sums of money for all of those devices, you simply pay for your smartphone which is a lot cheaper. The ability to create something that is cheaper than all other products combined means that knowledge is more valuable than most things. If you have the knowledge you can apply it to build something new and innovate. This process replaces other products or services of value and makes you even wealthier.

You could then say that devoting your time to acquiring knowledge is the absolute best use of your time. The return of that knowledge will come back to you many times over. Consider how Bill Gates, despite being busy improving healthcare concerns around the world and running a multibillion-dollar company, makes time to read books. Just the other day, he posted some of the books he had read in one month, even amidst the pandemic that was going on in the world. It is somewhat inspiring but also if you look you could find at least one hour a day to build your knowledge.

Therefore, I want to share some tools that will help capitalize on your knowledge and be used by multiple business owners to expand their capacity in their business. Some people who have been known to use these techniques include Oprah Winfrey, Warren Buffet, and Benjamin Franklin.

It's called the 5-hour rule and this is what is included:

1. Create mental space for yourself - Americans have been known to watch around 4 hours of TV a day. Yet that number does not include time on smart devices especially watching YouTube and other streaming services. Therefore, let's say the average American like Jamie watches 7 hours of entertainment on their TV and smartphone. This often could result in Jamie making unnecessary purchases and staying glued to his cellphone when that time could be used for other pursuits like learning, reading, and finding tools to gain knowledge. If he changes his habits, he can invest time in his business, buying the knowledge he needs to expand his business. The idea of creating space for yourself resides in removing distractions that are keeping you from gaining knowledge. Always be thinking about how you can acquire knowledge that will improve your business and your wealth along the way.

2. Plan to learn - Make no mistake learning is never by accident. Yes, perhaps at times you may have a learning moment but it will be a once-off aspect. What you need to do is make learning a consistent process. How do you make anything consistent? You plan for it. Let's take an example

in your business, perhaps you want to grow your skill set in leadership. To improve, you may need to read more books, enroll in a course, or get a mentor. Think about how much time and money that would take and figure out how you can carve that in each day. So, if you think about it in portions you will certainly be able to slowly but surely learn to lead your business in the right way. Another aspect I think you would get value from is setting goals for your learning. Make a note that you wish to master a leadership skill within a month or two and track your progress. Once you track your progress, you're more likely to commit and get more engaged in the process.

3. Read - I know we did cover this extensively but I want to share a strategy with you that can increase your reading and help you read more books in a month than you may have done in the last 3 years. It's about reading for at least 1 hour every day. Make it a priority in your day, do it early, and aim to read books related to business, that's nonfiction. Read up on business automation, or taxes, or business expansion and it will help you see new opportunities to grow in your current industry. Warren Buffet reads financial news for hours every day and that helps him to understand the investment and financial sector which he works in. When you start to read books that connect to your business, they will engage you and provide insights on improving your profits.

4. Experiment - Business is often about trying out new things that will grow your business. They say knowledge sticks when you make it practical. So, why not spend the time you are not watching TV or YouTube on applying skills you learned in your business and finding out the results over time. Thomas Edison experimented 1000 times before he figured out the light bulb. If you follow that thinking, your next best idea could lie in your next 1000 experiments.

All of the ideas above are how you can find time to gain knowledge and then apply it in your business. There are also many avenues you could explore to get the knowledge you need and I want to share some of the resources I use personally to learn.

TedTalks - This is an application that hosts some of the greatest minds of our generation who discuss topics that are far-reaching. You will find business talks from the likes of Simon Sinek, Steve Jobs and Tony Robbins. In the talks, you may find a spark of brilliance that will be the seed for the next idea in your business. If you invest 30 minutes a day to learn something new from TedTalks, it's easy to do. Multitasking is okay when using TedTalks, aim to get your dose of knowledge while running on the treadmill or taking a morning jog. Not only will it invigorate your workout but it will invigorate your mind.

Udemy - This is an e-learning platform that hosts courses on every type of topic you wish to learn. One of their popular courses would be to learn programming, and software development. Often business owners decide to learn this skill as it helps improve their attentiveness to detail. Therefore you can see it's not purely for knowing a new programming language. You can apply the attentiveness to detail in your business. Alternatively, you may wish to learn how to manage your taxes, time management, or even video editing. There is a cost associated here but it's minimal when compared to the value added to your business.

Coursera - This version of e-learning is slightly more advanced offering degree courses from online institutions. You could easily register and get yourself a business management degree which helps with the day to day running of your business. They unpack the details from being a leader to being an operations manager. It will show you how to think strategically for performance. This can be of great help especially to a new business owner who is challenged by the day to day running of business like tracking and measuring performance, setting goals, and running a team.

In this part of this book, the aim was to show you the importance of knowledge when owning a business, as well as to give you the skills and resources to help you improve your knowledge. It may take time and effort in the early stages, but with that, you will certainly start to see increased knowledge that can be applied in your business. It will soon be an important step as your business grows your knowledge will become even more useful.

Key takeaways

- Reading this book is not enough; you must apply the knowledge as it will help you run your business which yields profits long term. The habit of reading is a good one that will seek to support your knowledge base and keep you growing, and expanding. You will find that the knowledge you accumulate will make a difference for you and your team. Invest in books, courses, and seminars as a way to expand your mind, and make better connections.
- Knowledge of wealth can often be a controversial topic, but if embraced you will see that acquiring knowledge and putting it into action can truly enhance your business for the better. You will start to see that the applied knowledge helps you to create wealth, think broader, and improve your networks along the way. Many businesses find that their knowledge comes from on the job learning and that is also a good way to attain your knowledge. Even better is when you distribute your knowledge to your team so they can improve and grow.

- There is nothing more valuable than knowledge is a reality. If you can aim to read 50 books a year like Bill Gates, they will have the answers you may have been seeking all this time. While it may not be apparent on the first page but the more you read, the more connections you will make that can be applied within your business. You can leverage your knowledge and turn a small business into a bigger enterprise that consistently profits year on year.

Action steps

- Aim to watch a business video every 2 days on TedTalks. The videos could be an inspiring, informative or scientific video that can motivate you to make progress in your own company.
- Take action on your knowledge daily, do little acts such as sharing a post on LinkedIn for your business about the recent book you read or video you watched. This may be informative and inspire individuals who work within your organization
- Seek to make reading a habit. If you read 10 pages a day, you can easily read a book a month just like Bill gates.

There are so many ways to leverage knowledge, and when you choose to keep on taking action on your knowledge you can get great results for your business. Therefore, in the next part we'll look at how innovation can grow from the knowledge you take action on.

VI

Innovation

Innovation in business can be tricky since everything is moving so quickly it is quite a challenge to keep up. What is innovation to a business owner? This aspect is, of course, the age-old question that we need to answer.

Consider this. Imagine that every day you make changes and updates to your routine, your life, and you also start to notice how life also has many small changes that improve people's lives in society and the world we live in. Do you think perhaps that when you innovate in your business, it's about making an addition to your company?

Yes, you are always adding something to your current business model when you decide to innovate. This could be a new menu on your website or a new product range that has been requested by your customers. This is an innovation, and it can make a difference in how your buyers see you. As a business, you must always take the lead and charge through with changes and new ways of running your business. That's easier said than done and often takes deliberate effort on your part and a willingness to try and fail many times before you succeed.

You must keep in mind that you should innovate to stay ahead of the curve. That means that you should always be looking to find ways to leverage what other businesses are doing and apply this within your industry. It may not still fit your industry well, but you should be flexible enough to understand how to make use of it in a new and exciting way that delight your customers. Consider new technologies like voice, Artificial Intelligence, and creating a digital footprint that will enhance the reach of your business and keep you on the cutting edge.

You will learn:

- Why businesses don't innovate
- Practice modern business methods
- Find things that are trending
- Social media marketing
- Take advantage of the world we live in

Why businesses don't innovate

Let's start by first looking at why innovation tends not to happen, and then we'll look at how you can make it happen.

Lack of understanding - Business owners often does not understand the concept of using innovation in their company. You see others making use of innovation and reaping the rewards, but you aren't sure how to apply it to your own business and even where to start.

Vision is missing or not clear - Your business may not always be set in stone and have clarity. That lack of focus means you cannot pinpoint how and what to innovate within your industry. In that sense, if you are not sure what you are aiming for, you will always miss the target.

There isn't a benchmark for innovation - It means you don't have a way to measure your innovation standards, and what it could mean for your business. If you don't have a blueprint or model for success, it's hard to start.

Limited motivation - We may have touched upon this in the section on passion. Your business needs to be a driving force. If not, there will be little motivation for you to start to do more for your business and investigate ways to innovate. You will settle for the mediocre.

Limited knowledge of your industry - You may not have been networking and gaining the experience that sometimes can be the "secret sauce" for innovation. When you keep engaging and working with fellow business owners, there is a community that can lead you to new and better connections that help you discover new ways to innovate.

Practice modern business methods

To start an innovation culture, business owners must review if their company practices modern business methods. This could mean in the software, leadership, or communication in the company.

Dated management styles - Examples of this could be measuring office time and hours worked. The world is quickly moving to a more virtual workspace, and companies must embrace this new culture or be left behind. Your employees can work from anywhere in the world if they choose.

Many business owners are set in traditional models of leading people, where it was more autocratic, driving with a command and control style. This does not work primarily with the Millennials and Generation Z (Gen Z). Their preference is to have more autonomy and freedom to do their work in their own time.

An alternative to this would be training all members who lead people to understand a transformational leadership style that seeks to motivate and inspire people and help them do their best work.

Assess yourself and business - It used to be that business owners simply delegated the work, and there was less of a focus on personality and using assessments to understand your strengths and areas of improvement as a business owner. Modern-day practice dictates that self-assessment is necessary for the business owner as well as the people employed in your organization. In this way, you can understand what drives you and your team, and also focus on the areas that you are good at. This thought process will help innovation to thrive within your business. Aside from that, it will help you to grow as a leader and business owner.

Remove telemarketing - This is a sales tool with call center agents getting in touch with people who may be interested in your products or services. It can be annoying and frustrating to people, and it will even scare off potential customers. Word of mouth can spread, especially in the realm of social media, and before you know it, your business has a bad name. There are better ways to improve your sales, and it may involve reviewing your entire sales process, and creating innovations here. You could use email marketing or ads instead.

Encourage innovation - To encourage innovation in your company, it does need you to take the lead by building a culture of innovation. It could mean hosting connect sessions with employees and sharing the innovation strategy and building enthusiasm for the approach of change. It could also involve investment in innovation education to improve knowledge in your company. Your employees will be close to existing products and services and will have keen ideas about how to improve. You simply have to ask them, and they will suggest a multitude of ways to improve. Prime your teams to always ask questions and find out how to do things better at every stage.

Enhance business operations - In many ways, your business may be inefficient, and you may also not know how to remedy it. You can aim to improve this by applying quality management, stock control processes, and information management. How do you find these inefficient processes? You will need to consider using benchmarking exercises as a starting point. This means looking at other organizations in your industry and their performance and best practices. It's a good idea to model their best practices after doing a thorough internal analysis. You will find many ways to improve, such as automating your stock control, improving delivery times, and implementing more lean processes. The adage goes if you are not looking, then you will not find ways to innovate.

These are a few ways to enhance business by practicing modern business methods. It does take change, and with change may come many unsettling feelings for employees. Seek to manage the change before making any innovations. Know the reason you are making the changes so that you can safely explain to employees who may be reluctant to change.

Find things that are trending

Innovation is all about finding the trends and using them for your business. It's about introducing something new to your business even as the world is continually evolving. At the foundation of innovation is this innate need to question established models and habits in favor of better processes. Change is so prevalent in innovative companies like Netflix and Spotify. They are always pushing to do something that will shake the industry they work in for the better. As an example, Spotify recently signed a big YouTuber and podcaster for a lot of money. This has not been heard of before. At that moment, they managed to increase their share price due to the perceived value that the YouTuber brought into their company.

Let's consider a few other trends that you could use for innovation in your business.

Collaboration - There has been a massive shift in how people work. The old way was to work in silos. Some cliques always had the best projects and promotions. Things have changed where there is enormous scope for collaboration and co-creation. Decision-makers in companies can see the value of inclusion and bringing in the diversity of thought from all levels in their company.

You can also see this online as more crowd funding and crowdsourcing activities feature prominently in business. There is an internal form of crowdsourcing, as well as an external one. The internal version invites all employees to bring their ideas to the innovation table and be part of the project team that is making it happen.

This motivates people in the organization to share their thoughts, and they also get recognition for it and sometimes monetary reward. Externally, companies like Pfizer invite external individuals to send in innovative ideas, and if these ideas are chosen, they bring them into the company to run with these ideas. You can also use this concept within your business by engaging your employees in weekly innovation sessions and sharing ideas on how to improve. This shared ideal practice is beneficial and could be the next innovation in your business.

Innovation for good - Initially, innovation meant something within the tech space, with app creation being a favored way to innovate. This has become a space that is saturated now, and people are seeking ways to solve more significant problems in society. The first point is that a large part of the world's population is excluded from some of the innovation that has come to light like smartphone technology, automotive innovation, and more. There are many challenges in the world involving basic needs like clean water, air, and also poverty is rife in many parts of the world too. Innovation that focuses on this can be helpful to society and also improve your business along the way. It brings purpose to what your business offers.

Technology trends - Innovation does, at times, seem synonymous with technology. In reality, technology can enhance the process of innovation. The technology could mean many things, and the primary purpose is to prevent humans from doing menial tasks. We should use our brain capacity for greater things. It does this function well as technology has opened up the internet space where people have access to data without discrimination; information is no longer shut behind a pay wall for the most part. There is more inclusivity. Innovation can prevent overlapping tasks and repetitive tasks by removing them from your business process; there, it allows for more automation. The analytics can also be used to collect large amounts of data that can be used to make discernible trends to help businesses improve their process. In your business, using more technology to make things more comfortable is a part of innovation. Find ways that you can use this information to improve your business and innovate.

Social media marketing

You may have aspects like Facebook, Instagram, and YouTube spring to mind when you think of social media marketing. Yet, the world of social media marketing has opened up new ways for businesses to gain exposure when they decide to innovate. Social media marketing is how your business can use platforms like Facebook to connect with your customers and get them to interact with your brand. This, in turn, can increase sales and bring in more repeat customers.

The starting point is that you must create a profile on each of these platforms for your business. Generally, each platform is free, and it allows you to create and design a business profile. This profile acts as the front of your store and attracts people to link to your website and buy stuff from you. There are many tools to get more followers. You can choose to do it organically where you build your audience through engagement and commenting and growing. It may take some time. You may also start using paid advertising, which gets your brand in front of more people if you are willing to pay the price to social media platforms.

Along with that, you must create valuable content for your business. This usually means that you create content that is helpful for your readers and potential buyers. If you have a website, you may consider using Pinterest to drive people to your articles or blog posts and educate them on your product or service. Over time if they get enough value from you, they may consider making a purchase or sharing your content on Facebook. As more people share your content, it broadens your reach on social media platforms. This creates brand recognition and awareness for you.

Aside from social awareness and traffic from social media, you also seek to build authority with your business brand by showing social proof. People are more likely to trust big social media accounts and choose to buy from your brand. So it becomes essential that you build up your social media pages to give your customers confidence when purchasing from you.

Take advantage of the world we live in

I hope that this section on innovation gives you some food for thought, and you understand how much the world we live in has changed for the better. If you choose to embrace the power of innovation, technology, and social media, you will find that you can build up a solid reputation for your business. That will lead to you becoming the leader in your industry now and the future. Therefore, you need to ask yourself how to take advantage of everything available as a business owner. My first recommendation is that you always stay updated with current trends and somehow incorporate this into your business. Always be a part of the conversation by checking out trending topics on social media like Reddit and Twitter. These little steps will ensure you have your ear to the ground and understand the changes in the world of innovation. It's easy to get left behind, but as a savvy business owner, it's better to keep up, embrace innovation, and then become an innovator that is known in your industry.

Key takeaways

- Practicing modern business methods is vital to the future success of your business. Many businesses still get by using archaic technology and processes, but this is a short term solution that poses many risks. Modern business methods could include looking at new technology, software, and improved processes to help the efficiency of your business. It may be costly but will make a difference long term in how you operate.
- Finding things that are trending will be sure to bring you extra reach and revenue. You may find aspects that are trending by looking at your industry and what your competitors are currently doing. Yet, that's not the only point of research; you can find many sources of inspiration

from other industries. Think about how Steve Jobs would use his strange research places to bring ideas that would inspire new Apple products. He never wasted a learning moment, even if it was from his competitors.

- Social media marketing is sure to bring in new opportunities for your business. If you have not yet explored the digital landscape, it's time to start getting your business to have a loud voice in that arena. Often it could mean a massive learning curve for your business, but if you get in specialized people to support you, it will be beneficial and help you focus on your business at hand. Many companies are building authority and reach for your enterprise by embracing the digital world. They choose to build their brand from scratch and use a variety of tools like organic reach, influencers, paid to advertise, and more.

- Take advantage of the world we live in and know that innovation is the name of the game. Most companies are embracing the new world of innovation and being online. Use the technology and data that is at your disposal and create a name for your business. Consider that you no longer need to do everything on your own. The market has changed, and it embraces a shared value model. You no longer require employees. You can hire freelancers instead of projects and save costs along the way. Outsource your functions and automate your business with the multitude of software available just a couple of clicks away.

Action steps

1. Audit your company for archaic processes and technology. Make a list and find a way to eradicate those processes within the next year. It may take longer so also include that in your plan.

2. Look for trends by subscribing to business journals like Wall Street Journal and Financial Times. It may seem like an additional expense which may not be worth it but that investment is one that will help you see trends pop up and how to leverage those trends.
3. Think outside the box in every way, experiment every month with a new way of operating your business.

The term "innovation" is used to show the latest technology. The exact definition of business innovation is actually about bringing profits into a business.

There are many ways to introduce innovations, such as how you interact with customers, for instance, when Zappos is renowned for putting their customers first. Zappos' aim is to wow their customers when they call in.

It could be something little as mentioning their dog if they hear a dog barking on the call or something bigger like upgrading shipping for their clothing or handbags if it's for a special occasion. That is an example of innovation. What about Tesla, we know they make electric cars, but also they let their customers order their cars online without having to wait at a car dealership.

In doing these so-called little innovations, businesses become more efficient and forward-thinking in their approach. This could lead to more profits, as well. There are many practical ways to innovate. It all starts with thinking outside the box and wanting to improve the service to your customers. In this part of the book, I wanted to show you the value of looking deeper into innovation for your business. It is an opportunity for you to look at some key areas where you can also start innovating. In part 6, I will share more knowledge on the concept of reserves when managing your finances.

VII

Reserves

Building up reserves refers to seeking out suitable investments that will grow your company in the long run. Reserves could use your money as leverage, and instead of keeping it in a savings account, you could rather use it to invest instead. Investing is an excellent option to look at building up reserves. It shows that anyone can start from very little, build a significant nest egg for themselves. I'm sure that as you work long hours to build up your business, you also have hopes of taking it easy someday. You have expectations that you can retire young and retire rich, not having to worry too much about money, always thinking long term, and making money for you even while you sleep. Along our journey so far, we've discussed the growth of your business, which can take up to five years.

I would imagine that you built up your business to see those rewards, yet business has changed significantly. It is also about building sustainable income alongside your business. You may find that your business income fluctuates according to the time of year, or there may be political unrest that stops your business from working. You will always need a backup plan in case your business experiences challenges. You can end up making a safety net for your business until you can grow it, and it can stand on its own.

This concept of creating reserves will be one of the most important sections of this book, where you're often told how to run a business but not how to protect the income and expand that wealth. I've worked with many business owners who saw surges in their business but did not take the time or care to invest that income, and later down the line, it impacted their bottom line. In this part, you will see that our focus will be on investing in other businesses and considering buying other companies that will increase your equity share. This diversification in itself is a practical approach to growing your wealth, and doing it bit by bit is incremental, but it will add up to exponential rewards. When you're done with this section, you will have keen insights into money management and making it work for you. You will also have the tools needed to diversify your income while finding simple ways to invest in your future. Let's get started.

You will learn:

- Move money around
- Let your money work for you 24/7
- Know how to diversify funds into different accounts
- Tips for investing

Move money around

When discussing moving money around, this is best viewed from the idea where your business makes an income, and all of that profit is merely in your company account. The benefits sit within the bank account and earn minimal interest. This is technically a way to grow reserves in your business, but it's better when you use the right vehicle to grow your money. As a starting point, you will need to decide how much a sufficient reserve fund for your business is. This would take into consideration your goals for your business in 6, 12, and 18 months. Your business might be stable, and you may be seeing consistent profits month on month. In this case, instead of using the money on unnecessary aspects of your business, choose to use it to invest in the stock market or buy other companies that may add value to your company. An excellent example of this would be Microsoft. They purchased the LinkedIn platform a few years back, knowing that the world of work was becoming more social and knew they could leverage the user base in their business to participate in cloud computing and office software. Initially, the investment was significant, and they had not seen profits for years, but after a while, they started to make up for the investment through either profits or brand equity.

Once you start moving your money around in other ventures, you can monitor their progress and be diligent around those funds' performance. If you decided to invest in another company, make sure you are keeping your eyes and ears close to the ground about the operations and handling of the company. This can make a difference, as the leader will generally make a company succeed or fail. You can look forward to seeing upticks in your investment within 5-10 years or more.

Another option to make your money work for you would be to invest in the stock market. It may be true that many have tried and failed in this way to generate income, but I have not. To date investing in the stock market has yielded an excellent investment in companies like Amazon, Apple, and Netflix, seeing huge booms of profit year on year. The approach used would be to join Robinhood or TD Ameritrade, which is an online American Brokerage. Using their app, you can create an investment account for yourself. Start by connecting your local bank account to the application and freely transfer funds into your investment account with these brokers. They offer relatively simple tools to pick the best stock, and when starting, it can be educational learning about the top-performing stock.

If the stock market is not your thing, you may invest in other valuable items like art or gold. These are rarely seen as everyday items to invest in, but that doesn't mean you shouldn't investigate these aspects. They have been known to bring a high return on investment.

Let your money work for you 24/7

This is such a common phrase, but you may have seen it before, where many people say you can rest easy knowing your money is always working to create you more wealth.

The first thing you want to do is open a high yield savings account. This will serve to create an emergency fund in case there are a few challenges in your life. You will always earn a lower interest when you keep money in a savings account compared to when you decided to move to an investment account. A smart way to save your money is by using an FDIC-insured high yield account, which you can discuss with your bank.

You can then also decide to create streams of passive income used to define any money with little or no effort applied to gain it. Therefore, once you have set up your passive income streams, you can earn money while sleeping. Yet, that's not quite the words I would use. You do have to work for that income, but you do the work upfront. You will need to invest money upfront, which will come from your business profits or other savings.

This investment could either be time or money but can lead to substantial rewards down the line. The forms of passive income you may have heard off include real estate investment or having a partner in the business where you invest money but don't get involved in the day to day running of that business. This can be an interesting one where you become a silent partner, get your share of the profits, and do very little work. If your business generates a stable profit base and can become a silent partner, I recommend this option immensely. The scope for growth also improves so long as you thoroughly research it to ensure you are making the right investment.

Other forms of passive income could also be when you earn income from your business blog, YouTube, and social media. Your first point of reference should always be to run your business soundly. There is certainly no harm in building a significant social media presence and provide great content for your business, all the while getting excellent ad income along the way. This additional income can then be funneled back into your reserve account and invested in the business or invested in stocks, real estate, and other companies. Overall, you should always be thinking of your money doing the heavy lifting and making sure it does not sit around in your bank account when it could be elsewhere earning interest, profit, or dividends.

Know how to diversify funds into different accounts

What you must know about diversifying is that it's essential to spread your income across various investments. These investments could either be as cash, securities, shares, property, or alternative investments.

There is minimal risk associated with cash, but your money's buying power decreased over time due to inflation when it comes to securities like gilts, and overseas bonds have low risk, and the returns can be predictable.

Shares can increase your income if you invest the right way and adopt a buy low, sell high strategy. This involves looking for companies with a low stock price, but that are also reputable companies who are merely experiencing a downturn in that period. You then want to buy stocks in that company and hold onto the stocks until there is an uptick in the stock price. It may take 5-10 years, but there will be a high yield. Take, for example, stock in Amazon that was bought ten years ago. During 2010, the stock was worth $182, and had you invested in 100 shares; it would have cost $18200. Fast forward to 2020, and the stock price now at $2680 and those 100 stocks are worth $268,000. That could be the difference in your investment. Never underestimate the ability of a reputable company like Amazon or Apple to keep on growing. Also, always be on the lookout for more companies who appear to be on a similar trajectory, such as Zoom and creative company, Canva.

Remember to keep on building your portfolio regularly, and make it a monthly consistent practice of transferring funds to your investment account. Therefore when you see a great stock that will prove to be a winner like Apple or Amazon, you will have no problem acting on that stock. The idea behind this is that when you are consistent with your investment practice, it does not become a challenge to find large sums. You don't need to find large values because you spread the overall investment amount over a few months. This adds up, and your investment portfolio expands. In your portfolio, not all your investments are going to be a success. That's why I recommend doing as much research as possible and being diverse in your selection. In other words, do not put all of your eggs in one basket.

Learning how to diversify your funds is a fine art and a skill that must be mastered, but it does take preparation and insight to get there finally. Make sure you always keep an eye on those diversified investments and get out of the stock earlier if you can see, it is not performing well over an extended period. The best way to do this is to set up a monthly check-in on all your investments, look at each company and the current changes, look at the trends over five years, and consider the management of the company. You always want to know what is happening within those companies since it is your money that is invested in there. By following this type of painstaking process, you will learn when the best time to move over to your next investment is.

Tips for investing

Investing is certainly a helpful tool for any business owner. A savvy entrepreneur will find that when they invest in the right business, stock, or in themselves, the potential to extend their wealth increases. You will see this in the opportunities that open up for you when companies invest in and grow. You will also see this in the share prices after 5, 10, and 15 years and watch your money expand passively. There are a few more tips I want to give you to help when investing and building up those reserves.

Always have a long term view of your investments. If you look at your finances at this point, it will seem like it is performing poorly, but you have to force yourself to know that investments fluctuate and change, and only in the long run can you see the actual value of an investment. You should also keep improving your investment knowledge through reading more investment books aimed explicitly at entrepreneurs like yourself. If you read more investment books, it will motivate you, and you will be inspired to keep investing. You will look for more vehicles that could potentially yield a high reward for your business. Over time, you will also notice that you do not need to keep running your business to stay wealthy since your investments are working. You may then consider selling your business and creating a profit for yourself, which can also be invested. Entrepreneurs will always seek to manage some form of business, so even if you sell up your current business, you can turn to invest in companies that are not doing well, fix them up and help them grow.

This business investment will seek to expand your wealth more. The next stage of keeping reserves would also be to plan for expansion for your own company. Many companies invest heavily in research and development, bringing in the best people and technology to expand their business. This, in itself, is a good investment, as you are seeking ways for your business to stay on the cutting edge. You are seeking opportunities for your business to leave a legacy. This may even serve to be a motivating factor for you. You get to take a business that started as a passion project but turned into a multimillion-dollar company. Another opportunity that comes from building reserves is to retire and finally sell your business in favor of traveling the world. The possibilities expand as soon as you start to build your wealth within your company. You may find that your goals are too small for what you achieved now, and they need to be also expanded.

Key takeaways

- When we talk about moving money around, you can see that money is an asset you can use to build more wealth. When you start reshaping the way you view your money from your business, you begin to see that you've been sitting on a pile of wealth this whole time. The difference is making the smart moves and putting your money where it can have the highest chance of success.
- Money never sleeps, but you have to sleep. Understanding this, helps you let your money work for you 24/7. To

achieve this 24-hour work cycle for your money, you have placed it in the right vehicles that will help to increase those funds. This could be via investments such as other businesses, or buying other companies. You could also choose to invest in the stock market using the tried and tested methodologies I use.

- Know how to diversify funds into different accounts where you will generally have an investment portfolio. Instead of putting all your eggs in one basket, aim to move them around and invest in a variety of investment classes like property, stocks, or cash.
- There are many good practices for investing. These include diversifying your investments, avoiding the 401K or savings account, and finding companies where you can buy low and eventually sell high. These are sound business practices that will ensure you succeed and reach new heights in your business.

Action steps

1. Take some time to understand the various accounts you can move your money into that will provide better gains? Engage with your banker and find out the actual interest earned, and then seek better opportunities where storing your money becomes the ground upon which you increase it.
2. Download the Robinhood app to get started on investing and transfer monthly sums of money into the account so that when you do find the perfect stock, you will have the financial means to do so.
3. Diversify your portfolio by looking into an investment that is not currently in your portfolio. It could be a business investment or putting money into a stock.

This has been an enlightening section where you can look at building up reserves in your business. Many companies have reserves so that these funds can see them through when times become more challenging such as a financial downturn or political unrest. Since your business will not always have a great year, you have to ensure you invest soundly when the times are good. Therefore, making hay while the sun shines might be a cliché but is very apt. When your business is doing well, you will have the energy and enthusiasm to exert some effort in increasing your wealth and making your money work for you even while you sleep. It will take time, patience, and the learning curve might be challenging, but with persistence, you will find that you have built a diversified portfolio of investments. You would have created a great safety net for your family. You can certainly then look at retiring earlier than you planned or keep on running your business as a hobby. It always becomes more exciting to run a business as a hobby than when it is your bread and butter. Your business can use those secret weapons of building reserves to bring a sense of security to an otherwise insecure landscape all businesses face. You've passed the halfway mark on this book, and with a few more parts to go, I'm excited to share the ways that you can progress and keep building your business and yourself.

VIII

Progress & Build

In this part, my goal is to show you that you have to keep building your business consistently and not let complacency set in. You must always monitor your company's progress and find ways to evaluate your team's goals while setting goals for the new year. When you let in a culture of apathy in your business, then your organization is worse off. Apathy could be providing mediocre customer service or hiring average employees or even in not doing due diligence in every respect of your business. It happens that when a company gets successful, you start to see a sense of complacency happen within the firm.

This usually starts with the business owner, and slowly it makes its way to the managers and then the employee, and finally, it reaches your customers. How does it play out? You start to get complaints about your products or services, or the customer service level is not adequate. More than that, you will see that people are using social media to share their opinions, therefore creating a poor reputation for your company.

Companies that have a poor reputation find it challenging to get back their loyal customer base, and eventually, this can lead to fewer sales affecting the profit margins. It becomes more important to keep on progressing and building so that everyone in your company has a goal to work towards, they feel excited and invigorated in your company. It's true that when your employees feel engaged and happy at work, your customers do too. As a starting point, you want to evaluate how your business is doing. If you are a company that has not been monitoring progress, it may take time to get this discipline going, but you are fortunate that technology has made our lives very easy these days.

I'll soon share how you can track and monitor progress all in one place. The good news is that if you do it once, you build a vast system of proactively managing your business, and you need only check-in and updates it once a month. Once your business's administrative side is taken care of, you free up space in your mind to focus on other areas of your business, like growing your company and employees. You will endeavor to look for opportunities to improve and create a legacy with your company. Soon your company will be in overdrive, and the best way to keep moving on that momentum is by looking for teachable moments where something happens in the office then use it to innovate and grow. Teachable moments can be found everywhere if you would be willing to look for them.

You will learn:

- Tracking and monitoring progress
- Continuous improvement is key
- Look for teachable moments

Tracking and monitoring progress

Many companies must include some form of reporting and monitoring in their business systems. This is for many reasons. The first is to ensure that as the owner, you may have sight of weekly, monthly, and quarterly performance reports. Additionally, this data will help you ensure that your business operations are running well, and you can pre-empt any issues in the future. Any modern business needs a system that monitors, tracks, and trends their data, which will ensure that your firm is always audit-ready.

As a business owner, you are also responsible for managing the way your business operates. It could be in the form of reporting, standard operating procedures, customer satisfaction of financial audits. You then need to always be collating and building up reports which will give your team authoritative information. This will be related to spending, growth, and profits. Using this data will help you craft plans, budgets for the next financial year.

Additionally, management reporting is great for looking back at how far your company has progressed. You can view this year on year or even every month. Ideally, the reports should help you identify trends in your company, such as reduced customer satisfaction, product costs, or employee productivity. If you do see anomalies, you can quickly benchmark these based on your industries and investigate the irregularities. You can see how reliable data can be for a business, and when you eventually decide to sell your business, potential buyers may request this data. A standard tool that many companies are moving towards recently has included Qlik Sense or SAP. These tools offer an automated data solution for your company, often drawing out the data from your current systems.

Using the systems to review your business data and trends can show you any problems or issues that should be taken care of before they escalate. A company that simply uses annual reporting may be in for a surprise, as items only get picked up once a year when it may be too late. It could be creating problems, costing your company time and money where it could have been fixed a year ago. When you have an automated trended dashboard, you can view daily, weekly, and monthly, this will prompt a proactive approach, and issues noticed will be fixed swiftly. Opportunities for improvement also become highlighted, which may result in the future growth of your company, and we'll discuss more of this later in this part of the book.

Knowing the trended data will be useful in setting goals for your company. You can always set high goals that push your company and keep it competitive. These can come to be known as your Key Performance Indicators (KPI's), where your business also understands these goals and commits to meeting them.

Tracking and monitoring your business as thoroughly as you will help show many areas where your business may not be as efficient as you would like it to be. It may even show bottleneck areas where decisions are slow to form, and actions take longer, impacting your company's implementation capacity as a whole. Overall you can still manage your business using automated tools and other tools such as accounting software such as QuickBooks or organizational software like Monday.com. These tools are excellent if you are an entrepreneur who does not have too many employees. They offer you the opportunity to keep all your administrative tasks in one place and manage your team projects. If you are a business owner who wants everything in one place, this tool will be helpful. Alternatively, you may prefer to use all of the tools to your benefit, then that would also be recommended for you. Let's now set our sights on why continuous improvement will help your business progress.

Continuous improvement is key

Now that you have a firm grasp of the data in your business, there is more clarity on how well your business performs. You also have a keen sense of goals for next year and even five years. Your business is becoming more organized as you use tools to improve your company's efficiency. This is one step to improvement and progress. The next aspect is the continuous improvement, as in how you keep it going and get your entire team on board. It starts with the data where it can highlight problems you may not have seen without the detail. Even more than questions, you can shift the perspective and think of problems as opportunities in your business.

This ensures that you use those issues as potential innovations of the future. Data is great, but it is not everything. Some of the best improvements come from your customers and employees. Since your customers experience your final product and your employees are the most knowledgeable of your product, seeking out their opinions are vital. You can do this via surveys, social media, or giveaways that always bring more people to share their views. At the office, focus groups are great for leveraging ideas for improvements. You may find that your employees have the next iteration of your product in their head. A good tip is to actually use the ideas that your employees share and also bring them onto the project team as a reward. This not only broadens their resume but keeps them engaged and contributing.

I've shared a strategy about continuous improvement from employees and customers, but what about your competitors? These companies can be the most significant source of inspiration for growth. You can always observe their business using their social media, website presence, and the available data. This information will give you the sight of what could be working for your competitors and provide you with something to consider. This does not mean copying, but understanding their successes and modeling that in a new and exciting way. The competitive spirit is beneficial for both you and your competitor.

Another area of continuous improvement is where you invest in yourself. This could mean in the form of learning more about business, attending a seminar on your industry, and also seeking out industry leaders that you can form a mastermind group with. You may find that being a business owner can be lonely; you need to have an affirming group of like-minded people in your court who inspire you to keep going. Many business owners are devoted readers and learners. They aim to read and learn about aspects that will bring improvement to their business. They set high standards for their teams based on what they learned, and support and coach their teams to meet these goals. A great tool you can use is to share the concept of S.M.A.R.T goals, which stand for Specific Measurable Achievable Realistic and Timebound. This is a helpful way to structure your goals for your company. Let's take an example where you want your company to reach $500,000 in revenue for the next financial year. You would then state your goal using the SMART formula as:

We will create $500,000 in revenue by 31 Dec 2021 by adapting more efficiency in our business through data trending.

You can then see that the goal is more refined, you know exactly what's needed and when it needs to happen, and the only thing missing is the "how," which are the tactics of your goals. So using this goal-setting approach can help focus you on the main goals of your business that will be impactful. You may consider making this a visual statement on your dashboards, calendars, and even T-shirts related to the company. The next step would then be to look at ways to achieve this goal. You may look at your data and find that you offer a shuttle service for employees; however, only two people use this service. Questions can be asked, is there a more cost-effective way to provide transport to our employees. So by asking that question, you can already generate answers that can reduce expenses.

Look for teachable moments

Business owners can tend to take failure to heart, and let it get to them. That can be very demoralizing, so I propose that we switch the narrative and approach failure as a teachable moment. What do I mean by teachable? It's the ability to draw out a lesson from that business failure and make it into something that will be better for your company. Whenever I consider the concept of failure, I'm prone to look at the light bulb iterations. Did you know that Edison tried almost 1000 iterations of the light bulb until he could get it perfect? During that time, society relied heavily on gaslight, which was fuelled by kerosene. Kerosene had to be extracted, and it was dangerous too. It also meant that you always had to have some form of a lamp within your home if you wanted light. This was a highly inconvenient process, and Thomas Edison decided to take on the problem of the electric light bulb. He had tried a variety of filaments until eventually settling on bamboo that was treated to burn much longer. Now, of course, we use more resilient materials. This shows that he would keep learning with each failure and found the teachable moment that presents them. Imagine if you did the same in your business. It's possible, especially if you have a challenging customer who has rated your product poorly and impacted the sales.

Instead of blaming the customer, what if you had to approach it in a manner that looked at the complaint from the customer's perspective? You may find that you start to find empathy for the problem, and start asking questions that teach you something about improving your product. If one customer has these issues, there could be hundreds more who would love to solve their problems. If you adopt a mindset where you will be in teachable mode, your employees will feel more comfortable with failing and learning.

You start to build a culture that embraces failure and knows that with every failure comes an opportunity to improve.

There are many more places that you could find teachable moments. An excellent place to start is by connecting more with your employees; perhaps you have a team that is consistently giving great work. Another group does not have the same quality of work resulting in your products sent back for refunds that cost your business money. If you look at this problem, there is a teachable moment here. The first is that a synergy exists between a team performing well versus one that is not. You may be prone to ask the well-performing team for ideas that make them so successful. You may be inclined to bring both teams to the same area and also build good relationships between the team leaders. This ability to foster these relationships will help both sides. The first team will get a mentoring opportunity and a chance to help, while the second team will get an up skill. Your team leaders will have the opportunity to build their network.

When your business operates from a place of learning, then when something happens that was not planned in the company, people are more equipped to take a step back and ask:" Why did this happen," and this will prompt solutions that don't lie in blaming other areas or people. It becomes more of how we can solve this problem together.

Finally, the last part of teachable moments knows that you will not always be right. This can show up in many ways, as the business owner you fear being wrong or being upstaged. This can be so counterproductive to your business aims. Your employees know you are not perfect and prefer to see the human side of you as their owner. They want to know that you are teachable, that you are continually growing. It makes them more likely to follow you of their own accord. Some businesses opt to create teachable moments, a planned session where individuals will get together and share challenging moments that stretched them, and how they overcame those moments. They will often support each other or play devil's advocate in a situation. In these sessions, you are likely to draw great ideas for improvement in people management, processes, and customer engagement. Teachable moments are all around; you must look for them and be sure to share them.

Key Takeaways

- Tracking and monitoring progress is one way of finding bottlenecks in your business and quickly moving to a more efficient workplace for everyone. As the business owner, you may even find that you are the bottleneck when it comes to decision-making ability. This could lead to you creating more autonomy for your employees when making decisions.
- Continuous improvement is vital in a business where you should never stick with being complacent, for that's where mistakes creep up. Simple ideas can come from your employees, and it's about taking the time to listen to your team and find ways to implement their suggestions. When you involve your employees in the process, they become more committed to the company's goals.
- Look for teachable moments where if something wrong happens in the company, make a note of this and then create insights for your company. Always use the mistakes as lessons or stepping stones to more significant opportunities. If your company fosters learning instead of a fear of failure, people will be more prone to develop better ideas and build better products and services.

Action steps

1. Build a shared drive where your company's performance is updated monthly, and keep on giving your employee's sight of how the company is doing.
2. Host a top-performing ceremony to celebrate the milestones in your company every three months, and be sure to reward your top team members. They embody your organization's values and culture.
3. Create space for people to bring ideas that get executed. Create rewards for improvement such as days off, remuneration, or learning experiences.

Progressing and building your company is all about your dedication to constant learning and improvement. Every company has a unique character, and this is created by the employees that make up that company. Be thinking about what your company represents, how far you've come, and how far you still need to go. Let the progress you've made inspire you, but let the goals drive and motivate you as well. You will find that a highly engaged business owner wants to continually monitor progress, knowing that it may seem tedious at that moment. Still, it will be beneficial in the long term. If you are always monitoring progress, it also engages your employees who may be target driven. Like it or not, many people perform better when they have goals to work towards. It is even better when the goal is a company goal. These goals serve to build your company as people want to do better every month. Soon, your organization will be cultivating the idea of continuous improvement every day as well as embracing those teachable moments, knowing it will help the company grow. Our next chapter will focus on automation. Once you've built your business, it's time to embrace the world of making everything simpler, faster, and more efficient for your customers and employees.

IX

Automation

This will be a good lesson for the rest of the company that will drive even more improvements. When businesses automate, they make the lives of their employees and customers more comfortable. In this chapter, I will discuss how to automate your business and then expand it or sell it at a profit. You will get a sense of the best methods to sell and get the best deal when selling your business. Automation is not always for big companies; it can be for small companies too. Remaining competitive has become a way of survival for businesses where not automating could lead to your business losing steam and your competitors taking over.

Automation often happens when you want to reduce costs, become more productive, and bring better service to your customers. When you find a process to improve and then automate, you may find that it leads to unintended improvements in other areas of your business. In a way, you can see automation reverberates through your company and it starts by implementing the first idea, or getting in touch with the new software company or buying better hardware. These facts can be part of the solution, but automation is a complicated business issue that needs experts.

Ultimately, I'll show you how little actions can make the most significant difference in your business. This will update how you think about process improvement, seeking always to find better, more streamlined ways to do things in your industry. Steve Jobs was ousted from his own company in the '90s and went to Pixar, Apple performed poorly during that time, and they asked him to return. When he returned to the company, he noticed how archaic the processes were. That's when he started to get a reputation as being obsessed with the details in his approach. What people don't realize is that he began to get into the detail to find ways to improve the Apple business. He kept on asking the right questions and being nosy as to why people were performing a process in that specific way. He watched people work. He was running a multi-million dollar company, but he was close to the details of what his business did as ever. He looked at their operating systems and updated it to the NeXt operating system, which he had brought over to Apple. Those little changes in process and automation built into the business in customer service, in manufacturing and distributing, made a world of difference. Apple went back to its former glory but even better this time. You may be wondering what Steve Jobs has to do with your small business. I think there are many lessons to be learned about automation from big business. Since they have the funds to do thorough research and development, they often update and automate to align with the findings. If you watch them closely and apply their ideas and principles on automation, you start to think in that way too.

You will learn:

- Find ways to automate your business
- Make money in your sleep.
- The ultimate goal is to build a machine
- Sell your business

Find ways to automate your business

You can quickly find ways to automate your business by looking for the most straightforward processes first. Seek out those tasks which are mundane for humans, and that adds very little value. These tasks likely take up time and are frustrating. Since they are frustrating and repetitive, they tend to cause human errors. Examples would generally include data capture or a 24-hour call center, which can be time wasters and a drain on resources.

Make sure that you are not merely the one person in your business that is thinking about automation; make it a company-wide endeavor, and get people excited about the thought of automation. Many times, people fear that their jobs may be impacted by automation, but it's the complete opposite. They will not have the opportunity to do more substantial work. No matter how many organizations automate, there will always be work for people to think through complex problems that machines cannot figure out. Many aspects, such as leadership roles and consulting, are still needed. Therefore your communication as a small business owner is critical. When you talk about automation, also let your employees know about the benefits. Show them how other roles become available, and business process improvement will become a place where jobs of the future will soar.

Try not to do too many things at once. A good rule of thumb is to focus on function in the beginning. Look at the tasks that are costing a fortune, and start with mini processes in that function. Make little changes and build up the confidence of your teams in the automation process, and soon you will start making bigger, better changes along the way. One example is using chatbots instead of having customer service support standing by 24 hours a day. Chatbots are quite popular, but they are also becoming niftier and niftier. Not only will they help your customers but also your employees with the questions. One such example is Spoke, a smart bot that you can send your questions via slack, email, or SMS. It quickly uses the programmed knowledge to give you the answers you need. It uses AI to draw out more insights after each request so that it mostly gets smarter when you ask it a question.

Business owners often think that automation has to be a massive project; in reality, it can be smaller ideas that turn into the automation of processes. Since processes are connected, it can lead to older processes becoming redundant and resulting in massive value. In every company seeking to automate, there will be people more predisposed to automate, empower those individuals instead of feeling insecure about their knowledge. Send them to spaces that need more automation and where there is more waste. Eventually, you will have your whole company thinking of ways to improve processes and systems. Don't underestimate the power of putting proper methods in place and that these systems can cost money but will yield many profits in the future. Don't forget to build a process log of your automation, which will serve as a blueprint for improvement in the future.

Make money in your sleep

The ultimate goal for your business is to build a machine that will continue to drive revenue streams for you infinitely. When you, as the owner, leave the company, it should still work and stay for generations that come. An excellent example of this is Procter & Gamble, which has existed for close to 200 years. They brought you products like Pantene, Vicks, Oral-B and more. Initially, when the two brothers joined forces, one who made soap and the other candles, they did not foresee that their business could land up being the most lucrative business of the century. They were automated as much as possible, where they created factories where their goods could be manufactured, built standard operating procedures, and found better ways to make their products.

How did they automate?

The first point of contact was to engage their customers through surveys, focus groups, and now social media. They always wanted to know what their customers thought and especially what they thought could be better. Where suggestions were given, they found a way to create those products. Soon the demand became so high, so they had to find ways to improve their productivity.

They then branched out to other areas of the globe that needed more economic support and cultivated a space for proctor and gamble to manufacture. It was those simple ideas, and ways that they improved their productivity that made Proctor and Gamble the titan it is today. Their company relies on the process put in place to generate income, and the owners of this company do make money while they sleep. While this may be a huge business, there are some lessons you can apply to your small business. The first lesson is that you should always be leveraging your customer's opinions and turning them into better processes to automate the business. When you think of automating, sometimes it's not the process but also the technology which may be found in other areas of the world.

Ideally, you should aim to have a team around you that takes the pressure of and is thinking about improving your business. Even so, you should also be looking at the new technologies that are coming up that could serve to ease the workload. It might be that if you are a business owner with limited employees, then all the work will lay on your shoulders. Think of better ways to run your business. Leverage the resources in the world that can help you. You may consider buying software that will improve your invoicing system, or financial software that does all of your accounting for you, or even software that will help you manage your business. Some also choose to build a tool from scratch for their business, hire a programmer, and make your business software, which is the central repository for everything you do. This could be a good option if your business has particular needs.

Sell your business

Once you have automated your business, your end goal starts to change. You start to quickly shift to a mode of keeping your business forever to trying to sell up and go for greener pastures. Perhaps you always wanted to be a baker, and since it did not offer much in remuneration, you did opt to go in the business field. Now that your business is doing well, you think about your hobbies and how you can get back into it. This all becomes possible when your business is running like a well-oiled machine. It becomes the next step in your business process, and before you start to become disengaged in your business, you must find out how to get the best deal for your business and that often means selling up and taking the profit to invest in the next venture. In this case, automation is all about upgrading your business so you can improve your lifestyle.

The best methods to sell your business include finding its value. You will need to have your financials in order. If you've followed along in this guide, your financials will be in order and ready for assessment. Yet there is a big difference in selling on your own and doing it via a broker. A broker knows the ropes and understands precisely what is needed. It may cost you some money to use a broker, but at least you will have support on the process in terms of best practice and what to look out for. Brokers have likely helped many business owners sell their business before. They know the pricing range and also how to show the best side of your business.

A good starting point is to assess everything you know about your business. This means be realistic and thorough in your assessment. Being realistic could mean that you realize your business cannot be sold. It could also mean that you can sell it for a higher price than expected. Consider that a company is sold in terms of profit. But what are considered small, medium, and large deals? Smaller deals are up to $500,000, medium deals range from $600,000 to $1 million. And naturally, your larger deals would be a million dollars and upwards.

Using these calculations may not always get you to the best figure, so apply some logic and start engaging with other influential people in your industry. Keep in mind that if you have been in business for at least one year or more, and there has been a consistent upward trend in your profit margin indicating business success - you may have a company that will attract a sale.

To physically sell your business, you can go through 3 main places, and I have highlighted them below for you:

Bizbuysell.com is said to be the internet's largest business for sale marketing. Their website advises this. If a user on the service wants to sell their business, they can. It's quite simple as you would need to list your business on the site, and there is a small fee involved to access this option. From here, you can have your business shown to many buyers looking for a company that fits their criteria. Users have rated the site well, and have found speedy results, saying they had their business sold within seven days of registering on BizBuySell.

Bizquest.com is similar to BizBuySell, as you can also browse for business as well as set up your business for sales. As a seller on the site, if you post an ad, you get exposure on websites like wall street journal and the New York Times. If you'd prefer to go through a broker, there is an option to do so. They do get around 300000 visitors each month, and there are no hidden fees either.

Alternatively, you can look at Empire Flippers as another option. This website specializes in helping business owners buy and sell their online business. It's listed as being one of the top spaces to buy and sell established companies. They have a proven track record, selling thousands of websites with an 88% selling success rate. They do, however, need to know that your company has a solid track record of earning $500 of profit or more per month. They will also look at your company's website, specifically on Google Analytics, to get a sense.

Ideally, Empire Flippers connect buyers and sellers of business and ensure that the deals get done in the most effective manner, where no business owner is disadvantaged in any way.

Key takeaways

- Finding ways to automate your business is not easy, but with diligence and patience, you can do it. You will feel the changes as it seeps through into your business, freeing up your time, and helping you to be more strategic to grow your business.
- Making money in your sleep is one of the things that will come to mind when you automate. All that hard work you put in upfront starts to pay off as you quickly improve efficiencies, there is less need for you to be reviewing every process. It's about maintenance and looking at data points that signal challenges.

- The ultimate goal is to build a machine that can be your business model since when you create a machine, it practically runs itself. A business is not efficient when it needs you to do everything manually. It prevents you from truly stepping away, and it becomes more challenging to sell where you, as the owner, are needed to run the business.
- Hopefully, selling your business is the end goal you wish to see where you get multiple offers to purchase from serial entrepreneurs. They see potential in what you built or want to incorporate your company in their own company. You can quickly sell your business on broker sites like empire flippers or BizBuySell.

Action steps

1. Make it a goal that you will automate your business in the next 6-12 months. When you set this goal, make it smart, and also add to the benefits of automation.
2. Make a list of all the automation opportunities in your business, and then prioritize that list using Pareto 80/20. 20% of your actions and ideas will yield 80% of the results. Rank ideas according to Pareto and make a top 10 list.
3. Audit your business book by yourself or hire an accountant to help you. This will come in handy when you decide to sell your business.

Automation is usually synonymous with fear as more and more companies turn to automation to save costs and improve efficiency. As a business owner, it helps to lean into automation since your business needs this approach to stay competitive in almost every industry. Finding ways to automate does not have to prove too tricky, especially when you have the data and the trend, which leads to better processes. The best automation is the simplest. In your time working in the business space, you will come across entrepreneurs who always seem to be on the cutting edge, and it's easy to look on in wonder and hope for the best. The key to automating is to start with a simple process and work your way over to the more prominent means. Be the type of owner who always has their ear to the ground in your company. You can choose to be curious, investigative, and listen to both your customers and employees too. In doing so, you may find at. First, it will be hard to change and automate. It may even be more expensive as you invest in better technology and staff. If you can stomach those challenges and keep going, it will prove worthwhile as you start to see the rewards downstream. As you discovered in the opening of this chapter, automating business can be challenging, but companies like Apple have also gone through the challenges and come out even more durable. At first, there will be people who don't appreciate the changes, and it will create fear as it did in Apple. Still, by continually keeping goals top of mind and communicating expertly, you can change the way people view automation in your company and keep this a thriving theme as you keep on going in business. This can be embedded in the culture of improving, and as your company grows, everyone within also takes up the mission to automate.

Let's consider the final chapter, where you get to use everything you learned to finally launch your business.

IX

Launch

You have now reached the final part of this book. You will get to take a look into the procedure for starting a business from scratch as well in this chapter. This will help you see that starting a company has been more simplified over the last decade, where it used to be a long and tiring process that was also expensive, how things have changed. When you think of starting a business early, you may have thought that it would also cost your fortune, but over time and reading through the pages of this book, you've seen that it can be done quicker than you thought possible.

Let's summarize everything we have reviewed so far and then move onto the definitive steps to get started.

Sacrifice

Initially, when you start a business, it will involve significant amounts of sacrifice from you and also the people closest to you. What does this mean? Well, time will undoubtedly be a considerable investment in the beginning, and that may become a commodity that you simply do not have. You have to give it everything you have and see tiny rewards in your business's early stages. It helps that you know this at the outset, as it will prepare you for what's to come in the future. Additionally, make sure you research the business thoroughly beforehand, as it's essential to know all of the risks before leaping. If you've done this and given the planning phase your due diligence, go ahead.

For many people, money can be a reason for starting a business. We all crave to have additional income to buy the things we want and do everything our family desires. The money also means that you have to think about how you fund your business in the beginning since there will be many costs associated, such as investing in assets in your business, paying salaries, and unexpected expenses that could show up along the way. If you are patient about generating a profit, that can also help. Ensure that you do not always spend all the profits immediately on personal aspects such as getting a flashy car until your business can be sustainable and create benefits long term and consistently.

Another factor is that you may no longer have any weekends or free time, as everything will be devoted to running your business. If you've invested money into your business, that is not enough. There is some level of effort required in the early stages and means working longer hours where you are away from your family. It will not always be the case, but always discuss this matter with your significant other when taking up the idea to start a business since it is such a huge commitment. If you are running the business on your own, you will have to be the primary driver within your company, so your enthusiasm and energy will have to be high. This could mean that other factors that drain your energy will have to take a back seat. Being the CEO of your company also means you are the captain of the ship responsible for everything that happens, bad or good. You must take responsibility both for yourself and for everything in your business. This generally means that you have to make the best decisions using all the information you have. You have to keep on being proactive and take action every time. Mostly you are the business, and the company is you.

Passion

You discovered passion is a foundation for your business. If you go into a business venture with very little enthusiasm for what you are about to do, you will regret it. Being passionate will show up in how you eventually run your business on a day to day basis. It will also show the type of people you attract into your company. This can lead to either a world-class organization or one filled with mediocre attitudes and people. Radically you must love what you do and enjoy business because you will be doing this for long periods with minimal rewards. This can take a toll on a person when there isn't a passion for the work. That's also where your goals come in. You must set inspiring goals that keep you moving forward. It could be writing down your goals daily or visualizing, but you must have a way to wake up every day, ready to hit the ground running. When you think about owning a company, does it inspire you? If so, then this will be a sign that you must keep on stepping in that path.

Team effort

A team can make or break a business. If you hire the right team with the right mindsets, your business can build significant momentum. During the early stages of running a business, make sure you know exactly what is needed for your company to perform well. You cannot always be a one-person show. There comes a time when your skill set will not match, which will drain your energy and time.

Additionally, it helps when you hire a team of professionals to work with you. If the best people surround you, then you instantly improve your odds of success, they will get the job done in the right way, and there will be less need for micromanagement. You can play your role of being an owner in the company and keep on being strategic. You can quickly find great people by getting in touch with your networks, looking through LinkedIn, and other social media platforms.

Many business owners forget the aspect that leadership skills are vital when running a business, especially when you are running a team. You must know how to handle people and when you seek to see the best in people, giving them care and treating them with dignity, they will respect you more for it as they go above and beyond the call of duty. Therefore, don't be the boss that people don't like and who makes the workplace toxic. Be the boss that people will gladly follow even if you were not the boss.

The key is to being likable and approaching people in a manner they appreciate. It will help to remember that we are all human beings who feel empathy. Be empathetic and get to know about their interests and this will help significantly. Most importantly, be authentic and help people improve and get better at their jobs.

Knowledge

The good thing about reading this book is that you have taken a keen interest in running your business. The next thing is to apply that knowledge, so it helps your company generate a profit sooner. Gaining experience is predictable as you simply need to scope out great books and build reading habits. It will seem like a chore, but later on, you will grow to love reading once you start seeing how it improves your ability to connect the dots in business.

Do yourself a favor and invest in knowledge like books, courses, and seminars. In this way, you will see that knowledge can help you create long-lasting wealth. Knowledge is power, but only if you apply that knowledge. Become a business that uses education to their advantage and make sure that your team is constantly learning and growing

It's true when successful business owners say that there is nothing more valuable than knowledge. This knowledge accumulates, and even when your business may not have done well, you can always find the knowledge to bring it back. Your knowledge grows when you grow, and so too does your potential for wealth.

Innovation

If you operate your business now, you can longer survive using older processes and technology as it will only serve to cripple your chances for success. It puts your company at direct risk when you choose not to upgrade your business where you get left behind in terms of process and efficiency. Modernizing your business may be costly at first but will pay off in the long run and keep your business being sustainable. This is one way to embrace innovation.

Another way is to actively search for trending aspects in business, which will help to bring you more reach and income. This is often apparent in your industry trends and what your competitors may be focused on. Look at all forms of research and take inspiration from every arena, including blogs, videos, and online learning.

Social media is another avenue for you to explore. Since there are billions of users on Facebook, Instagram, and TikTok, you must build your brand and grow. You must always take advantage of the world we live in, where every innovation is published and shared with a global audience. Use this knowledge to bring inspiration to your company.

Reserves

Keep in mind that money is an asset that can be used to build more wealth for you. When you think of your business and create reserves, you are mainly planning for your company's future. In this way, you can control how you expand your current finances, and you can choose to grow your income from your business by using a variety of vehicles. Understanding that money never really sleeps makes you more aware that you have to make your money work for you while you sleep.

There are many ways to do this for yourself in terms of investing all profits of your business instead of splashing out or splurging. You could choose to invest in the stock market, or buy companies or real estate. A great tip that I shared with you is that diversifying that income is vital so that you don't have all your assets in one basket. Keep on reviewing your investment month on month and making changes as you go. Some of the best advice I've received is to avoid the 401K for your savings and opt to invest in companies using the strategy of buying low and selling high. When you choose to build those reserves, you make a self-sustaining insurance net for yourself and your family. The sooner you start, the better.

Progress and build

Once you've considered the various stages and phases of operating a business, you may find that when applying the tools I've shared so far, your business gains momentum and starts to see a profit. This is good news and means you are doing something right. You must keep going and be consistent. It's also a great idea to track and monitor your progress using business reporting to your advantage. This is one way to see where there are bottlenecks in your business and where you can improve.

You can only do this when you commit to unpacking reports, looking for trends and anomalies then making plans to fix processes. The name of the game is continuous improvement, and it is the enemy of complacency. If you commit to incremental improvement every day, you're committing to growing your business and bringing your employees along for the ride. Finally, when you start to progress and build, you will see failure every single day. If you choose, it can derail your entire company, or you can use it to get better and improve the way your business operates. If something happens, that is not optimal, take note of this and use it to innovate and learn from it. Make your company a place filled with teachable moments.

Automation

If anyone told you automation was easy, they might have been misled. It sure is a challenging process filled with many highs and lows. Despite being so challenging, it can lead to many cost savings and better processes for employees and customers. You have to start small, though; it's better when you make incremental updates to processes or systems instead of large ones. In this way, it allows you to manage the change better and monitor the effects of automation. Speaking of change management, if you have a business that has employees, you must keep reminding your employees that automation does not necessarily mean job loss. It means that you remove redundant tasks so they can perform more complex tasks. When you automate you free up time for your business to think more strategically and be more innovative, yes, it will indeed be so much hard work earlier on, and that has to be paid up front. Don't be discouraged as you will be rewarded when you start earning more profits directly from that automation, you will mostly be making in your sleep. Your goal is to build a well-oiled machine that functions without you. It runs itself, and you simply need to make checks once in a while to see that everything is performing as predicted. Automation has one other benefit, and that is, you can sell your business because it will be more efficient and profit-generating, which is attractive to potential buyers. Platforms like Empire Flipper and Bizbuysell make it even simpler to advertise your business and link you to a suitable buyer.

You now have the blueprint for starting your business and running it until it makes a profit. Perhaps you noticed that I have not yet covered the practicalities of getting started. This is by design, as I wanted to share the foundations of being a business owner first and then show you the exact steps getting started.

How to get started

Now that you have a good understanding of all the concepts we have discussed in the previous sections, it's time to give you a general procedure of how to start your business.

Register an LLC: The first step is to register an LLC, a limited liability company that offers more protection if your business fails. For most new business owners, this is the best option, and you can start by forming the LLC in the state you live or where you will conduct all business. There is a rule that says if your company has offices or sales reps in other countries, you need a foreign LLC. Be sure about the location, so you get the right LLC. Many experts start their LLC in business friendly places like Delaware or Nevada, where their laws are more in tune with businesses. It does cost more, so keep this in mind.

It's important to know that you need to use a registered agent. This person understands legal matters and can help you through the complicated process of getting the LLC set up. Some examples include legal summons and filings that may not be familiar to you.

Almost every state says it is mandatory to have an agent to support you in this process. You can then officially create your LLC by filing your formation document with your state. Finally, once registered, you will need to get an Employer Identification Number (EIN). Think of it as a social security number for your business entity since you will need this number to employ people and also for you to get a business bank account. The best place to quickly get your EIN is directly via the IRS website.

Get a company account: Once the paperwork is sorted out, you can move on to getting a bank account for your business and separate personal income from business income. If you mix your personal and business income, you put your assets at risk.

Know your tax: It's also a good idea at this stage to get a tax agent. Many businesses register their tax information too late and get into trouble later down the line. To avoid this, remember to make it easy for yourself and deal directly with a tax agent who is an expert in these matters. A tax agent would be an accountant who understands the intricacies of tax returns, so you don't need to.

Establish your brand: Now that the administrative aspects are out of the way, it's time to get into your business brand. You can easily create your business brand and logo if you are creative and have the right software. To start with, you must know and understand your target audience by truly identifying who your business will serve. Feel free to do research online on Facebook groups, Reddit, and Quora. Once you know the target audience and who you will serve, create catchy slogans, and choose the colors that best suit your company by using Adobe or Canva. Easily have your logo designed on Canva or hire a freelancer online to do it for you. You should swiftly apply your branding across your business including your website, social media, and documents

Build your website: If your company does not have a website, it will not be visible to potential customers. In this step, you must go ahead and create a website. There are 3 top platforms that you can make use of, including Squarespace, WordPress, or Wix. Keep in mind. You will need to pay a monthly fee to host your website on these platforms, as well as a fee to register your company domain, such as "Thepaycycle.com" or "Business101.com". Many domains are taken by now, so it helps to think of an original name, and always get a .com address which has more authority and is also trusted more. When building your website, if you make it using Squarespace or Wix, it is much simpler where you simply design using their drag and drop features. On the other hand, WordPress is more powerful, and if you get a good theme and invest time into learning how to design it, your website will be more professional.

Social media presence: Once your website is up and running, you have to find ways to get people to find your website online and buy what you are selling. Since social media has so many users, it's the perfect place to set up your business and link to your website. Start by creating social media accounts on leading platforms like Instagram, Facebook, and Pinterest. Make sure you use your logo and brand colors in each of these platforms, which will bring consistency to your business, and also, people will trust your business more. Think of social media as your storefront in different locations, where your website is the head office. The aim is to entice your potential customers on social media and get them to your site. It takes 5-10 minutes to set up on each platform to get started. Aim to post once every three days by educating potential customers on your products or services. Aim to educate and inform, and this will draw customers to find out more about your business. Remember to add a link to your website on your social media page.

Facebook ads: Facebook ads are also an excellent way to bring customers to your website to buy your products or services. You can quickly set up an ad account and run inexpensive ads to create brand awareness. Your first campaign should be to build up your engagement on Facebook and improve your page's likes. If you run an awareness campaign, you can quickly build up 10,000 followers on Facebook within 3-4 months. Once you've done that, create good content that your followers enjoy and connect with. Make content that entices people to read more on your website. Once you have done all of this, you can create ad campaigns that bring people directly to your product pages, where they can make purchases.

Set up Google Analytics: Google offers to report on the visitors that view your website. The information includes time spent on your website, pages viewed, types of visitors and their location. This is a free reporting tool that can be linked to your website, and you can view it daily/weekly/monthly for any trends that could help boost your business.

These steps are the building blocks for getting started on your new business venture. If you have applied these steps, you can see how easy it is to register for your business. I also want you to keep in mind that there are so many more aspects of running a business that must also be considered, and that will help you to thrive. Your passion and commitment will be crucial as you progress and build towards a better future for yourself. You may now see business as a stepping stone to reaching your ultimate goal, but I can assure you that it can be a challenging task ahead with a steep learning curve. It's so important that you look into your current levels of passion for the business you started, and consider how you can cultivate that passion day in and day out. My advice is always to keep your goals top of mind, make it visual, and celebrate the small wins.

Those small wins can be motivating, especially in the early stages, when your business has not seen a profit for months. I would also like to be upfront with you and tell you that starting a business is not for the faint of heart. The fact that you took the first step by reading this book, and began to take actions means this is something you are interested in, and it is worth pursuing. You are standing at the best time in entrepreneurship. It's where anyone at any age without care for their background can start a business from the comfort of their home. All you need is a good idea, passion, follow-through, and a WIFI connection to get started. You will need some form of investment for expenses to get the website and domain name going, as well as to hire employees if you need help.

I can recommend that you save up the funds before starting, and then when you start, you have less worry about a lack of funds. Perhaps you are not at the point where you have a full-time job and need to manage both a business and a job. Many people will tell you to quit your job and make your business your priority. I don't recommend doing that unless you have substantial savings to see your through for at least one year. If you have that, you are very fortunate because you can get started today by registering your company and building your website. If not, there is still room to start if you have a job, which can be the tool to help you fund your business. You can invest monthly to get your company registered, then start saving for expenses and a year of income so you can eventually quit your job. If you do this incrementally, that can also be helpful as you create milestones for yourself, where month one you can get registered, and month two can be when you get a website and domain, and month 3 is a designer for your brand and logo.

I mention these options because I wanted to show you that there are many ways to get started based on your current situation. You now have all of the tools needed, so the next step is to consider the best next level that will match your circumstances. Then, take that step and monitor the progress. Once you've completed that step, take the next step until, at some point, you will look back and see how your business started at $0 of income and now makes more than $100,000 of income every month.

I hope that inspires you to get started and take the first step towards being a business owner.